Southampton
SOLENT
University

LIBRARY

Risk-based Auditing

For Margaret, without whom this book would
not have been possible.

Risk-based Auditing

PHIL GRIFFITHS

GOWER

Reprinted 2008

Published by
Gower Publishing Limited
Gower House
Croft Road
Aldershot
Hants GU11 3HR
England

Gower Publishing Company
Suite 420
101 Cherry Street
Burlington
VT 05401-4405
USA

British Library Cataloguing in Publication Data
Griffiths, Phil
   Risk-based auditing
   1. Auditing, Internal 2. Risk management
   I. Title
   657.4'58

   ISBN 10: 0 566 08652 2
   ISBN 13: 978 0 566 08652 6

Library of Congress Cataloging-in-Publication Data
Griffiths, Phil, 1952–
   Risk-based auditing / by Phil Griffiths.
      p. cm
   Includes index
   ISBN 0-566-08652-2
   1. Auditing, Internal. 2. Risk management. I. Title.
   HF5668.25.G74 2005
   657'.458--dc22

                                                                        2005014423

Typeset by Bournemouth Colour Press, Parkstone, Dorset.
Printed and bound in Great Britain by TJI Digital, Padstow, Cornwall.

Contents

List of Figures

List of Tables

Introduction

Risk-based audit is probably the most exciting and significant development in the Internal Audit profession's history. It has the potential to catapult the reputation of and the value added by this profession into the stratosphere.

If it sounds a little far fetched for a group of 'checkers' and 'nit-pickers' (NB this is still a common perception amongst audit customers) to reach these dizzy heights, this book attempts to provide the evidence. It is my intention to explain and demonstrate how risk-based internal auditing can directly enhance an organisation's profitability, image and social responsibility and help it avoid nasty surprises.

Internal Audit is not new, of course. Indeed the profession officially began in 1941 when the Institute of Internal Auditors was formed. For the first 50 years of its life the practice of internal auditing, arguably changed little from the compliance and review focus, which was its original raison d'être – as confirmed by the many hundreds of organisations with whom I have dealt during the past decade.

Since the early 1990s there has been a conscious effort by leading Internal Audit functions and the profession itself to refocus and re-brand its offering. The aim has been to add greater value, focus attention on process and systems rather than transactions and also to work together with management rather than to try and find them out.

It is clear that progress has been made and that the profession has progressively become an attractive option for career-minded individuals, rather than being viewed as a backwater with little opportunity for advancement (as it was sometimes regarded).

Our own research, however, which was initiated six years ago (primarily targeting Chief Executives), indicated that the role of the function was still not well understood nor properly appreciated by key customers. Indeed our original survey of the FTSE 250 Chief Executives in 1999 revealed that only 44 per cent of the recipients were positive about their Internal Audit function (and 27 per cent were openly critical).

A selection of the actual comments made illustrates the problem:

'Useful low key function'

'Good at basic financial and admin checking'

'Improving but needed to'

'Image is rather slow and methodical'

'Not really integrated into the business'

'Not viewed as a key group department'

What Internal Audit needed was a shot of adrenalin. This was to come a few months later.

The timing of the 1999 survey coincided with the launch of the Turnbull Report on Corporate Governance, which set out to change the way UK organisations managed and reported their activities on behalf of their stakeholders. At the core of the Turnbull requirements was the need to demonstrate the active management of risks and report on this subject to the shareholders.

The Combined Code disclosure requirements looked at from a dispassionate viewpoint could simply be regarded as a need for listed companies to sign off the disciplines and processes already in place. However, the resultant debate and its intensity suggested that companies were far from happy to do so.

The fulcrum of this debate was risk management. Most businesses believed they understood and could manage their significant risks, but the list of well-publicised failures and problems has demonstrated that such issues are not always fully understood. As a result of the governance reforms, risk management grew in just a few years from being a useful tool to become the very pulse of the organisation and the way in which management of an organisation is increasingly judged.

No wonder tensions have been created. It should be no surprise that many Boards of Directors were uncomfortable in being asked to certify that they had reviewed the significant risks within their business; stakeholders, after all, would be quite entitled to ask 'If all the significant risks have been reviewed (and presumably appropriate actions taken to mitigate them) why wasn't the recent problem anticipated?'

It was clear, therefore, that the Board needed help, not just in reviewing the effectiveness of internal controls but also in providing assurance that all the significant risks had been effectively reviewed. Furthermore, ongoing assurance is required to ensure that the risks are being fully managed and an embedded risk management process is in place. This was always going to be a tall order. In many organisations this challenge was passed to the Internal Audit function. The other assurance functions within the business such as the Risk Management, Compliance and Insurance were increasingly also being given responsibilities in this regard.

The challenge is not just for PLCs either. Public sector senior management are now very aware that similar governance responsibility falls on their shoulders and are reacting accordingly. Corporate Governance is also likely to become a pan-European 'hot potato' very shortly as pressure to integrate the different corporate governance codes across Europe intensifies. The challenge is therefore to 'raise the bar' to provide much broader assurance than ever before and audit the things that really matter.

This book aims to explain the concepts and practice behind this best practice approach – and demonstrate that risk-based audit is much more a mindset than a process. If you asked the question a few years ago 'Why did the auditors cross the road?' the answer may have been 'Because they looked in the audit file and that's what they did last year'.

It is increasingly recognised that audit functions that are able to focus their efforts towards the significant risk in their organisations are able to concentrate their limited resources on the issues that drive business goals and aspirations. In consequence audit plans are directed at the issues which really matter.

So, if you were to ask the question now of those who have adopted a risk-based approach, 'Why did the auditors cross the road?', the answer should be 'Because there was enough risk to make it interesting'.

1 *What is Risk-based Audit?*

The Internal Audit identity crisis

Let's face it, if you are reading this book, you are probably either already an auditor, preparing to become one or responsible for managing or overseeing the function. The other possibility is that you are considering a role in Internal Audit – if this is the case I hope to be able to whet your appetite and show you what a wonderful opportunity it brings.

Whichever category of reader you are the first major bridge to be crossed is the identity of the function.

I was to learn that we tend to meet any new situations by reorganising – a wonderful method for creating the illusion of progress

This quote by the Roman Caius Petronius in AD 66 illustrates the dilemma for Internal Audit.

Internal Audit has seemingly attempted a number of changes in approach over the years, but have any made a real difference?

Is Internal Audit seen as the 'White Knight' charging in full armour, past cheering throngs of well-wishers to rescue the damsel in distress or the 'Lady with the Lamp', splendid and serene, tending to the ranks of wounded in the Crimean War without a thought for her personal well-being.

Probably not.

It is more likely that an auditor may be seen, to use the old joke, as the team that comes in after the battle and bayonets the wounded.

The role still has somewhat of an identity crisis. Risk-based audit offers some, if not all, of the solutions.

In the following chart I would like to pose a question to you to illustrate the point.

Please pick the one creature which you believe best describes the role of Internal Audit in the eyes of the Chief Executive or Directors of your organisation. Try and put yourself in their shoes. If you asked them the same question, what do you believe their answer would be?

Let's analyse the most likely responses:

- Dinosaur
  If this is the perception, you have a major task ahead. You need to move quickly; otherwise you may become extinct.

- Snake
  The snake in the grass, waiting to trap the unwary, is a very common metaphor for the function in management's eyes.

What creature best describes how your function is seen?			
Ant	Cow	Goat	Porpoise
Antelope	Crocodile	Horse	Rabbit
Bear	Crow	Hyena	Sheep
Bee	Dinosaur	Jaguar	Sloth
Bull	Dog	Kangaroo	Snake
Butterfly	Dolphin	Koala	Springbok
Camel	Donkey	Ladybird	Stag Beetle
Cat	Duck	Leopard	Tiger
Cheetah	Eagle	Lion	Whale
Cockatoo	Gazelle	Praying Mantis	

Figure 1.1   What creature best describes how your function is seen?

- Praying Mantis
  This insect looks reverent and calm (the stance looking as though it is at prayer) but if a tasty morsel passes it, it is ready to strike and become a 'preying' mantis. Does Internal Audit give out these vibes? Outwardly innocent but a menace in disguise.

- Bee
  Buzzing from flower to flower not staying long in one place and a sting in the tail if things get really tough. Better than the dinosaur, praying mantis or snake but still probably not quite how Internal Auditors would like to be seen.

- Koala
  Let's be realistic, you are never going to be regarded with as much affection as the cuddly koala bear.

- Donkey
  Dependable, not afraid of hard work and has to carry many burdens – maybe not such a bad comparison.

- Ant
  A fantastic teamworker but small and easily trodden on.

- Dog
  Reliable, faithful and if it is a guard-dog, looking out for the business – a safety and comfort provider. Maybe quite a good metaphor – unless you are seen as a terrier snapping at the heels.

- Lion
  Strong, respected but can be very fierce and intimidating. Much better than the snake but probably not quite as you would wish to be seen.

- Dolphin
  Super-intelligent, sleek, fast and loved by everyone. It would be very good to be thought
  of as a dolphin. This is a very good goal for Internal Audit, although I am not sure if you
  will ever be loved by everyone.

- Eagle
  The very best metaphor for modern Internal Audit. The eagle flies majestically across its
  domain, able to watch over its environment and take everything in and when necessary
  can swoop down and deal with issues.

The risk-based audit approach is the tool you need to ensure that you are increasingly
regarded as the eagle or the dolphin.

Definitions and outline

So what is risk-based audit? It is a process, an approach, a methodology and an attitude of
mind rolled into one. The simplest way to think about risk-based audit conceptually is to audit
the things that really matter to your organisation. Which are the issues that really matter?
Probably those areas that pose the greatest risks. What else would you really want to review?
If your organisation has already identified its key risks then you already have the basis for risk-
based auditing. Clearly, if risks have not been formally identified and assessed then there is a
real opportunity for you to work with management to help create this information.

The second way of looking at risk-based audit is as a process. Traditionally audits begin
and end by looking at controls, often regarded as the main expertise that the function has.
The problem with this approach is two-fold.

Firstly, management do not *really* understand controls, which can be an alien concept
for them. If they do understand the nature of controls they tend to consider the need for
more controls as an unnecessary additional burden.

Secondly, it is unlikely that your Internal Audit function is an expert in control. Can you
really say that you understand the controls in all aspects and all activities within your
business? It is therefore necessary, if you are going to demonstrate your eagle-like qualities,
to be able to talk to management in a language they understand and appreciate. To fully
engage management you need to talk to them about something that is important to them.
If you start by discussing their objectives, what they need to achieve and how this is
measured you will attract their attention.

Having created the common ground (and it is preferable if you have first given some
thoughts to the objectives in the area under review before the meeting), you can now go on
to discuss the threats to the achievement of those objectives, the barriers to success; these
are, of course, the risks.

Again management should be able to elucidate many of the risks or threats, but
theoretically, if you have tried to anticipate the types of threat beforehand this will act as a
positive spur.

Having created an understanding of the objectives and risk you can then discuss the risk
appetite, the boundaries set by senior management (by authorisation limits and so on) or,
indeed locally, the limits beyond which the management of the function to be audited will
not venture (or is advised not to go) in risk-taking.

The next stage is then to discuss the processes in place to mitigate the risks already identified and those that appear on the horizon and the areas of concern or opportunity in relation to those processes.

You are now, of course, talking about the controls, but rather than doing so in isolation you will be discussing them as part of the full management process and should receive a much more positive response as a result.

The essence of risk-based audit is therefore customer-focused, starting with the objectives of the activity being audited, then moving on to the threats (or risks) to achievement of those goals and then to the procedures and processes to mitigate the risks. Risk-based audit is therefore an evolution rather than a revolution, although the results obtained can be revolutionary in their magnitude.

The chapters that follow expand these principles into a full process, explain the attitudinal changes and the broader range of skills required together with the tools and techniques necessary to adopt the process and to become a world-class Internal Audit function.

The challenges for Internal Audit

Figure 1.2   Do you recognise yourselves? Are auditors fighting the good fight? What could the big 'C' word signify in relation to the audit role?

- Control
  Ask auditors their prime area of expertise and many will say 'Control'. Can you honestly say that you are an expert in all aspects of your organisation's operations? I doubt it. Why then is Internal Audit obsessed with control?

- Compliance
This is an important aspect of the traditional audit role. It is still very important today, getting the basics wrong can spell disaster for organisations, but should compliance be the main focus of the Internal Audit role? Our continuing research with Chief Executives would clearly indicate that this is not the case.

  The question was asked as to the *prime* focus of the function. The respondents had to pick the approach that was primarily followed.

Prime focus of the function
Bi-annual Chief Executive's survey

	2000 Percentage	2002 Percentage	2004 Percentage
Business risk orientated	40	72	89
Financial systems based	23	7	1
Operational systems based	20	10	2
Compliance orientated	10	6	1
Internal consultancy	4	1	1
Value for money	2	2	0
Corporate governance	1	2	6

Compliance, as can be seen, is increasingly unlikely to be the prime focus for Internal Audit, with only 1 per cent of organisations who responded adopting this as the primary approach.

  As you can see, the prime focus is very definitely focusing on the key risks. This is not to say the other processes are not important, but they are unlikely to remain the dominant focus.

- Conflict
Hopefully Internal Audit does not get into too much conflict with management. Over emphasis on control and the failure to make recommendations that are 100 per cent practical can, however, lead to such a situation.

- Challenge
This is definitely a key role for the modern function. You need to question the 'we've always done it that way' mentality and challenge the status quo. If you do not do so in the course of an audit, who will?

- Co-ordinate
Wouldn't it be useful if Internal Audit co-ordinated its activities with the other assurance provider in the organisation, such as Risk Management, External Audit, Health & Safety, and so on. This would reduce duplication and create more focus. An approach on how to achieve such a co-ordinated approach is outlined in Chapter 8.

- Champion
Internal Audit should certainly be regarded as a champion. You have the opportunity to look right across the organisation and identify opportunities and good practice. Sharing such ideas is key to success and recognition.

- Catalyst
  The very best Internal Audit functions are regarded as a catalyst for change, helping the organisation through the difficulties of changing environments, cultures, and so on. Another key catalyst role is bringing people together to discuss areas of concern and opportunity, a best-practice agent.

There are others that you can think of, such as co-operate, convince, conscience, and so on, but I hope that the above have generated an indication of the trends occurring.

The trends

Having suggested that risk-based auditing is an evolution let me attempt to trace this change process. Let's have a look at some of the trends in risk-based audit. One question to pose is 'Are you fire fighting all the time or are you able to plan in advance?' The more fire fighting you do the less likely it is that your organisation is focusing on its key risks. If you are able to link in directly to your organisation's evaluation of risk, that's much more effective. The best way to illustrate the transition is to consider the different approaches to Internal Audit.

1 Compliance
   This is where Internal Audit began. It is still a valid approach but is rather limited in its focus, as it tends to concentrate efforts on whether or not the procedures and policies are being adhered to. Is that enough in today's challenging environment? I would certainly say that it fails to optimise the potential of the Internal Audit activity.

2 Systems-based audit (SBA)
   This is the approach adopted by more modern Internal Audit functions. The approach is predicated on evaluating systems and processes rather than locations or branches. Essentially the SBA is a horizontal rather than vertical approach, reviewing an activity across the organisation and looking for the areas where there are inconsistencies or interfaces are incomplete. Systems-based audit is therefore much less transaction based than compliance, indeed the phrase 'cradle to the grave' is often used to describe the process. The approach is to follow a small number of transactions through the system from start to finish to prove its effectiveness.

3 Risk-based audit
   Risk-based audit builds on the SBA approach focusing on the areas of the highest risk to the business and uses a different starting point, business objectives rather than controls. The recommendations made are also risk-evaluated to ensure maximum benefit and buy-in by management.

4 Value for money
   This is the review of a process to determine whether optimum value for money is being achieved and to make profit-enhancing recommendations. This audit approach was used extensively until a few years ago, but seems to have fallen out of favour. I believe that this is an excellent complementary approach to risk-based auditing and would suggest that it should now be a feature of most audits, to assess whether or not the activities

achieve the best value for money in your organisation. Certain audits such as travel costs, mobile phones and other items of corporate expenditure lend themselves particularly well to the VFM approach.

5 Assurance-based audit (ABA)
This is the most recent and some would say the real winner for Internal Audit functions. ABA is using the risk-based approach to co-ordinate all the assurance activities in the organisation to ensure that duplication is minimised, nothing falls between two stools and a co-ordinated assurance position is given to the Board. This topic is discussed in depth later in the book.

Changing the focus

As a way of being able to demonstrate how many organisations' Internal Audit functions still mainly focus on the traditional issues, let me share some statistics with you. When we ask Chief Executives and Internal Audit functions as to which areas they almost always audit, the answers are quite revealing. The five main areas they say are:

1 Adequacy and effectiveness of accounting controls.
2 Capital expenditure.
3 Physical security of assets.
4 Financial systems.
5 Systems under development.

The first four, as you can see, are the very traditional financially based activities whereas the last one is a much more positive trend, looking at new systems under development to make sure they incorporate controls and effective risk mitigation before the system goes live. The assertion in many studies on the subject is that it is ten times more costly to put in a control after the system goes live than beforehand. So clearly, this is a very positive area for Internal Audit to be involved in. I will return to this topic because some would say that this involvement could compromise Internal Audit's independence. I don't share that view and I will explain why later in the book.

When we ask Internal Audit functions which are the areas which they never or almost never audit, we get a very different list:

1 Corporate Planning.
2 Health & Safety.
3 Investor Relations.
4 IT Strategic Planning.
5 Human Resources.
6 Marketing.

As you will recognise, these are much more challenging audits but I would suggest they are the areas that probably represent higher risks to the organisation. Let's take them in sequence.

CORPORATE PLANNING

This is clearly a critical activity for all organisations. Failure to get this process right could be a road to disaster. So this is a sensible and logical audit to undertake.

HEALTH & SAFETY

It is clearly not sensible to duplicate the work of the health and safety function but is surely very valid to be able to look across the activity to assess its overall effectiveness.

INVESTOR RELATIONS

For those of you in private sector organisations, this is another critical issue; to determine how the organisation's shareholder relationships are managed. This is an activity which, in my experience, is very rarely audited.

IT STRATEGIC PLANNING

One of the most common reasons, in my experience, for recommendations not being accepted is that management assess that it would require a major system development or IT resource requirement which is not available. Therefore why not have an audit of how the organisation determines its priorities for use of IT resources and systems development.

HUMAN RESOURCES

This is a very important area for any organisation and should therefore be audited. There should not be any area that is off limits for Internal Audit and I would say carrying out an audit of a critical HR management area such as succession planning is usually a very interesting and very important audit. It is one that very few Internal Audit functions carry out.

MARKETING

How many Internal Audit functions would feel confident in going in to do an audit of marketing? This should not hold any terrors as marketing is just a process and auditors' main area of expertise is process analysis.

Let me illustrate this with a real-life example. In my previous life as Head of Internal Audit for a major retailer, we decided to carry out a review of marketing specifically to assess whether or not the organisation achieved value for money from its corporate advertising spend, particularly television advertising. I went in to meet with the marketing director and he asked a very reasonable question, 'What the hell do you know about marketing?' My response was, 'Not a great deal, but you do!'

The key point I was making is a crucial one for modern Internal Audit functions, as they move into more and more challenging arenas the less likely they will have expertise in that area of the business *but*, as Internal Audit's real expertise is process, then any audit should be able to be completed with confidence.

I therefore explained to the Marketing Director that we were intending to review the process for the measurement and evaluation of marketing spend with a view to assessing its effectiveness. We therefore embarked on a very different type of audit where we went out into our stores and we asked the public what had influenced their purchase, had it been the TV advertising, brochures in magazines or had it been the signage in the stores, and so on. It was apparent that the marketing function had a bewildering array of often-contradictory methods of assessing marketing success. As a result of the audit the measures were simplified and consolidated. One of the unexpected benefits of the audit was that it was clear that customers had often not even noticed the signage in the stores. Our recommendation was that the signage should be removed on a test basis in a number of stores to see if that made any difference to the sales. The recommendation was accepted and tested in ten stores and it was found that sales were not affected at all by the lack of signage. Therefore the signage was cut back significantly from all stores, saving a huge amount of money. Despite the earlier reservations by the marketing personnel we now became quite popular and we were asked to carry out audits of many other key areas of the business.

Institute of Internal Auditors professional standards

The Institute of Internal Auditors as the official voice of the profession has been championing the development of the activity for many years. The definition from the Institute of Internal Auditors has been around for a couple of years.

> *Internal Auditing is an independent and objective assurance and consulting activity that is guided by a philosophy of adding value to improve the operations of the organisation.*
>
> *It assists an organisation in accomplishing its objectives by bringing a systematic and disciplined approach to evaluate and improve the effectiveness of the organisation's risk management, control, and governance processes.*

A few of the key facets are highlighted below.

INDEPENDENCE

It is critical that Internal Audit is seen as an independent function. Internal Audit must not have any other role and certainly no management responsibility. However, if independence gets in the way of adding value, another of the key requirements as per the definition, there is a dilemma. I firmly believe that the spirit of the definition relates to independence of thought and relates therefore to objectivity, hence the reference to 'objective assurance'. Internal Audit must be shown not to be biased, not to be influenced emotionally or politically by issues which come up in the audit. Adding value and objective independent assurance are critical and complementary aspects of the risk-based audit approach.

CONSULTING

The topic which has generated a huge amount of discussion, the concept of the Internal Auditor as a consultant might appear bizarre to some. To imagine the auditor as the oft-used joke, someone who borrows your watch to tell you the time and then keeps the watch, would not be a positive view of the role. However, having the wider remit and freedom that an external consultant often enjoys could well be very useful. The main difference between consulting assignments and the other work is that I believe that consulting jobs must be requested. Such assignments will often be carried out in a completely different manner. It is now possible to carry out an Internal Audit by workshop. I have led a number of such 'audits' in my career. For example, if you are looking to audit a contract or a project or something with a start and an end, an excellent approach is to assemble the key personnel involved in the room at the same time and to ask them what are the things that have gone well to date, what hasn't gone so well, what are the threats and areas of opportunity. You can then determine the areas you wish to test, complete them and get the same people back together and present your observations or report back to them and (hopefully) get some agreement to actions required. This is a very positive experience for management and what is more, they don't even know they've had an audit. This is a very different type of approach and very much a consulting type of assignment.

ASSISTING IN ACCOMPLISHMENT OF BUSINESS OBJECTIVES

The next aspect of the Institute of Internal Auditors' definition is that it assists an organisation in accomplishing its objectives. As risk-based audit directly relates to achievement of objectives, this is an entirely consistent aspiration. The words highlighted towards the end of the definition are that Internal Audit helps evaluate and improve the effectiveness of the organisation's risk management, control and governance processes. Until recently this definition just referred to control – now risk management is referred to first. This again reflects the basis of a risk-based approach. The final key word in the definition is 'governance' and we will talk about this critical topic a little later. A second definition, one which you are probably not aware of, resulted from a piece of work done under the auspices of the Institute of Internal Auditors a few years ago to develop a competency framework for Internal Audit.

Internal Auditing is a process by which an organisation gains assurance that the risk exposures it faces are understood and managed appropriately in dynamically changing contexts.

The definition is very different and appears 'light years' away from the compliance orientation. This definition, whilst not formally adopted by the Institute of Internal Auditors, has been incorporated in part in their standards (2004 update). The wording is as follows:

Performance Standard 2600 Resolution of Management's Acceptance of Risks

When the chief audit executive believes that senior management has accepted a level of residual risk that may be unacceptable to the organisation, the chief audit executive should discuss the matter with senior management. If the decision regarding residual risk is not resolved, the chief audit executive and senior management should report the matter to the board for resolution.

The implication is that Internal Audit should be looking at all the key areas of risk and how they are managed and, if Internal Audit believes the organisation has taken unnecessary risks or has risk exposures, which are unacceptable or too high, these should be discussed and agreed with management. As you will notice, the Institute of Internal Auditors standards state that, if there cannot be an agreement, this must be reported to the Board – a significant opportunity to influence at this level.

WHAT IS BEST PRACTICE?

Is it possible to define best practice Internal Audit? I am not sure you can do so easily. One way to explain best practice is that this is the process adopted by the most respected and successful functions.

We have developed a database of best practice based on information from over 3000 Internal Audit functions worldwide and when I refer to best practice in this book it will reflect the practices that the best follow and how they do so. One very clear message from such functions is to 'forget the petty cash', a euphemism, of course, not only for the petty cash but all minor issues, the issues that don't really represent significant risks to your organisation. Someone could take the petty cash everyday and it wouldn't really make a great deal of difference to your organisation, would it? It clearly does not mean that you should never audit these areas but make sure you keep such reviews in context and to a minimum.

RECOGNITION AND REPORTING LINES

Make sure that you are able to operate at the very highest levels in the organisation. If you are not having regular contact with senior management including the Chief Executive it is very difficult to know what the key issues are. A monthly meeting of the Head of Internal Audit with the Chief Executive is regarded as good practice plus a quarterly meeting (at least) with each of the other directors.

GETTING IN AT THE START

Internal Audit needs to be able to demonstrate its willingness to add value and work with management. An excellent way to do so is to offer to advise on key systems under development. It is much more valuable to identify areas of omission or controls needed at this stage. You will not be thanked if you identify these issues three months after the system has been implemented.

I have heard concerns expressed about Internal Audit being involved in systems development projects – the argument being that this might compromise independence – 'how can we be involved in the project and then come in after implementation and audit the new system?'

I do not believe there should be any concern. Providing Internal Audit acts in an advisory capacity and is involved at key stages only and does not sign off the system then independence cannot be compromised. It is a critical aspect of the independence that Internal Audit should not be a signatory to systems, procedures or any other development. If they sign-off such activities then they are part of the process and their independence is inevitably compromised.

A further aspect of getting in at the start is to try to be ahead of events. If you can sit down with senior management and explain that you are planning an audit of a key topic and this happens to be the most important issue in his or her mind, you will be seen as proactive and the reputation of your function will be enhanced. Indeed the key issue in terms of risk-based audit is to look forward not back. You will get no credit for critiquing the past when management are facing the challenges of the future. Increasingly this will take you into 'the crystal ball' areas where there is little history and there isn't a lot of information, for example, e-business or e-commerce. But what an exciting area to be involved in!!

What is the role of the function? Policeman, risk assessor or consultant?

What is the role of the Internal Audit function in the modern era? Is it to police, is it as a risk assessor, or is it as a consultant? The general view here is that it has to be a combination of all three.

1   The role of police officer is not considered a very sexy image for the Internal Auditor but there has to be an element of policing in any Internal Audit role. The policing aspect is probably reducing but it must still feature in the role.
2   Risk assessor definitely features heavily in the modern audit role. An independent assessment of how well the organisation is managing its threats is clearly a very significant and important role.
3   Consulting, as we have seen earlier, is becoming a much more important aspect; indeed a completely separate set of guidelines are included in the Institute of Internal Auditors standards for professional practice. If you are trusted enough to complete a consulting assignment when the option is to engage an external consultant, then clearly that has to be an excellent vote of confidence. You have the capability to do a great deal within your Internal Audit role. Have confidence!!

How Internal Audit has developed

In considering the development of the Internal Audit profession, there are four distinct stages.

*   Stage 1 Traditional
    The earliest and most traditional approach was a very detailed, often painstaking, audit focused almost exclusively on financial activities and which was totally compliance based and involved reviews of frighteningly large volumes of transactions. In fact, in some organisations, including banks, this type of audit was referred to as an inspection. Thankfully most Internal Audit functions have moved on from that very time-consuming approach. The biggest concern looking back was that in years gone by, Internal Audit were often part of the process (and not totally independent) because they were required, for example, to review and approve payments before they were made. This, happily, has been recognised as the management function it always was and passed over to them in almost all organisations. This convenient 'crutch' for management has now been despatched to the archives.

*   Stage 2 Systems Based
    The next development within the Internal Audit function cycle was establishing a systems-based approach. Rather than focusing on individual locations, branches, and so on, you should audit the processes and systems looking across the organisation, a horizontal rather than vertical approach. The systems-based audit (SBA) approach

focuses on adequacy of controls rather than reviewing large numbers of transactions. SBA is recognised as much more constructive and collaborative.

- Stage 3 Developmental
  This is the modern approach to Internal Audit whereby you can and should audit any function in the organisation. A risk-based approach is adopted, focusing on the activities that really matter to the organisation, concentrating on the objectives rather than the controls and looking at the threats to their achievement. The emphasis is now on the overall business framework rather than individual systems with a view to identifying areas where accountability could be blurred, for example, where interfaces between functions occur. This is where most audit functions should be operating or at least should aspire to be.

- Stage 4 Forward Looking
  The final stage is to be even more forward looking:

  1 Looking for and getting requests, particularly for consulting-type assignments.
  2 Being regarded as a solutions facilitator rather than a function pointing out problems.
  3 Operating as a business partner, or maybe even an advisor and a mentor. This is the most positive role for Internal Audit and is the ultimate deliverable from the risk-based approach.

Summary

In summary, the essentials of risk-based auditing are widening the coverage, tackling some of the non-traditional areas and focusing to help management achieve their objectives. It requires a demonstration of greater knowledge of the business and, more importantly, allows a much broader level of assurance to be given to the Board. All these ideas are expanded in the subsequent chapters.

2 The Need to Understand Risk

Approaches to risk management

To truly embrace risk-based audit it is necessary to consider the meaning of risk. This is a term which is very widely used but often misunderstood.

Definitions

The first definition I offer was developed by the Economist Intelligence Unit, a UK government department:

The threat that an action or event will adversely affect an organisation's ability to achieve its objectives and execute its strategies successfully.

This definition highlights a number of key factors:

1   A risk is invariably a threat – something that might happen.
2   The threat relates to an event – something that has to occur for the risk to crystallise.
3   The event, if it occurs, will impact on achievement of business objectives.

The one aspect of the definition which I dislike is the word 'adversely'. Risk does not necessarily impact objectives in a negative way, it can be positive. It is for this reason that I prefer the definition that comes from the Australia/New Zealand Risk Standard, the only internationally recognised standard relating to risk management. The definition in this standard is:

The chance of something happening that will have an effect on business objectives.

In addition to the benefit of being a simple and readily understood definition, the word 'chance' is a very good one as chance can be positive or negative. This is a very good way of being able to define risk.

   Another good explanation particularly looking from an Internal Audit point of view is that risk can be seen as the pulse of the organisation. This is a very good analogy, and auditors, to continue the analogy, are there to take the pulse. You need to ensure that your organisation embraces the issue of risk, managing rather than simply tolerating the threats and, therefore, missing the opportunities. I firmly believe that risk management should be considered a positive process, risk is not just what can go wrong, it is better to think of the things you have got to get right. You can (and should) help to provide management with the required assurance that the risks are being managed effectively.

Wrong assumptions about risk

Here are some wrong assumptions about risk, each of which I have heard:

1 '*Risk is only something for finance and insurance to worry about*'. This is clearly untrue, risk is everybody's responsibility; everybody can and should be seen as a risk manager because each employee has objectives that need to be achieved.
2 '*Risk comes up on the agenda once a year*'. A very big mistake made by a number of organisations was to regard risk management as a 'tick the box' exercise. Risk management is not a passing fad and clearly risk is not like Christmas, it doesn't just happen once a year, it is a continually evolving and changing process. As the organisation changes so does the risk profile.
3 '*Business risk management is just another layer of unnecessary bureaucracy. It is just another initiative*'. Embraced fully and enthusiastically, the opposite is true, it is a way of reducing bureaucracy, identifying the unnecessary controls, identifying areas that are over-managed or over-engineered, creation of value rather than failure.

How misunderstanding risk can spell disaster

Some of you may remember Ratners, the jewellery empire and its charismatic owner, Gerald Ratner, when he had his ill-fated 'off the record discussion' with the press and he described the products and services he sold as 'crap'; he brought his company to its knees very, very quickly.

I worked in the retail sector at the time and went to a presentation Gerald gave to other retailers a week before the above 'faux pas'. The same sentiments expressed there were clearly recognised as a joke, but not so it would seem by the public who did not like to be considered idiots.

Think of Perrier a few years ago when they had the scare with contaminated product; in some parts of the world it was dealt with brilliantly, in others it was a total nightmare. Perrier thought they had a consistent process for dealing with such crises, but they did not. It took them over 18 months to build back market share.

Think about Barings Bank, how one rogue trader brought down a bank. Think of this demise from an audit point of view. Leeson said in his book that when an inexperienced auditor was sent out to Singapore from London:

> *I didn't know what the auditor knew but I realised he was asking me a question rather than accusing me of fraud and wrestling me to the ground and, that if he was asking me a question, he might not know the answer. So I made something up.*

He said it made no sense at all but it was the best he could come up with under pressure. He apparently had to pinch his leg under his desk to stop himself from laughing as the statement was patently ridiculous but the auditor believed him.

The key issue is that auditors need to be prepared and aware of what an appropriate response would be. Be very wary of sending inexperienced auditors on critical assignments.

Then finally, think of Andersens, the highly regarded auditing firm that had been established for 80 years, and suddenly disappeared in a flurry of allegations of document shredding post the Enron scandal.

All the above examples relate to trust or loss of this precious commodity. There are, of course, the more positive aspects of risk management; think about the first moon landing in the late 1960s, can you imagine the risk associated with that programme? Had there not been a moon landing, however, we probably would not have microwave ovens in our kitchens, and we certainly would not have Teflon coating on our pans and many other benefits that came from the moon programme. So it is good that some of us are willing to push the risk barriers back.

Surprises and risk

Any organisation that has encountered unwelcome surprises or unexpected losses will realise that most were preventable.

Such events will almost certainly have been caused by risks that were not fully understood, or the processes to mitigate those events being inadequate.

Do you agree with the above statement? It is widely recognised that most surprises are caused by risks which are not properly understood or the procedures, controls or other processes to mitigate the risks not being effective.

An excellent way to begin a risk-based audit is to sit down with the management of the activity to be audited and ask them about the surprises they have had in the last year or two. You should also ask about any near misses. Asking such direct questions will also be a surprise to them and you will generally get an honest response.

Learning about surprises, whether these are positive or negative in nature equips you well. A pleasant surprise is just as important to discuss because if the reason for the surprise is not known, next time the impact might not be as favourable.

During the audit, you can then evaluate the actions put in place to reduce the likelihood of their recurrence and hopefully provide comfort to management in this regard.

Risk and culture

One of the most important and least understood areas impacting Internal Audit is the culture of the organisation and its attitude to risk. It is essential for the audit function to establish the organisation's risk culture, whether it is predominantly risk averse or risk embracing and whether the culture is perceived to be the same in the area under review as at corporate level. If the culture as set by senior management is risk averse but certain functions are very risk embracing, this can create conflict and confusion. The opposite scenario is equally fraught with danger.

I will describe the two main risk cultures (although in reality most organisations tend to be some combination of the two).

A RISK-AVERSE CULTURE

In this type of organisation:

- Management tend to stick with what they know; stability, experience and knowledge are the key values, and are the attributes most highly regarded.
- This organisation is very reactive, it tends to wait until something goes wrong before acting. It is usually extremely hierarchical and most decisions have to be made at the top of the organisation.
- The primary focus of such an organisation is inward looking, management spends most of its time working on how to do things more efficiently and more effectively, rather than focusing on what the customers really need.
- In this type of organisation, strategies don't change very often, and when they do, it's a big event.
- Mistakes are personalised so that people don't put their head above the parapet in case someone comes along with a big stick and knocks it off. It is a typical blame culture.

On the other hand, there is a risk-embracing culture. This is sometimes called a 'can do' culture. There is an easy guide to assess whether your organisation is risk embracing. If audit recommendations are made and management respond with 'let me tell you 28 reasons why this won't be successful' or 'we tried it three years ago and it didn't work', you probably have a predominantly risk-averse culture, whereas, if they say 'Good idea. Let's have a look at a couple of ways that might work', you are probably risk embracing. In a risk-embracing culture:

- Innovation and motivation are the most highly regarded values.
- Trying to exploit opportunities and empower people, the decision-making ability is passed down the organisation. The primary focus in this type of business (typically known as customer-focused) is external.
- Strategies and policies change regularly to reflect changing circumstances.
- Making a mistake is quite acceptable – even encouraged – covering it up is definitely not.

It is really important to understand the culture or sub-cultures of your organisation because, clearly, if you are a risk-embracing culture and you have pockets of resistance, you will need to challenge this thinking with your audit observations. It is just as important to identify the risk-takers in the risk-averse organisations because they could be either loose cannons exposing the business to unexpected threats or entrepreneurs identifying opportunities for the business. Either way the approach to the audit and the recommendations you make will need to reflect these situations. We will discuss the challenges in later chapters.

Risk management policy

INTRODUCTION

Risk is the chance that an event or action will affect an organisation's ability to achieve its objectives and to successfully execute its strategies.

Risk management is the process by which risks are identified, evaluated and controlled

– the extent to which the organisation responds positively to the opportunities faced whilst at the same time understanding and seeking to control any factors that could prevent its success. The aim of risk management is to improve awareness of the consequences of risk-taking activities, reduce the frequency of damaging events occurring (wherever this is possible), and minimise the severity of their consequences if they do occur.

Risk management and internal control are firmly linked with the ability of the business to fulfil clear corporate objectives. By embracing risk management in this way it will help to ensure that we focus on opportunities as well as dealing with possible threats. It is therefore essential that risk management be embedded in the planning process. It is also important to demonstrate a consistent and co-ordinated approach, ensuring that there is documentation to demonstrate accountability and openness.

Because there are well developed business planning and financial planning processes in place, a more formalised risk management approach can be included seamlessly into these processes and managed as part of the current reporting mechanisms.

There are many benefits to embedding risk management into the organisation's culture including:

- greater management focus on the issues that really matter;
- reduction in management time spent fire fighting;
- fewer surprises;
- more satisfied customers;
- protecting reputation;
- more focus on doing the right things in the right way;
- greater likelihood of achieving business objectives;
- fewer complaints;
- increased likelihood of change initiatives and project benefits being achieved;
- more informed risk taking and decision making;
- support for innovation;
- lower insurance costs.

The objectives of the Company's approach to risk management are to ensure that:

- managing risk is a key part of the strategic management of the business;
- there is a positive approach to risk taking;
- risks are considered in all key decision-taking;
- opportunities are maximised by actively managing the risks and threats that might otherwise prevent success.

To achieve these objectives, the Company will adopt the following approach:

- Clear accountabilities, roles and reporting lines for managing risks will be established and maintained across all functions and departments.
- A programme of training and learning opportunities will be introduced to enable managers to acquire and develop the necessary risk management skills and expertise.
- Risk assessments will be incorporated and considered as part of all decision making, business planning and review processes of the company.
- The measures taken to manage individual risks will be appropriate to the likelihood of

occurrence and potential impact of those risks on the achievement of the business objectives.

- An up-to-date risk register, readily accessible to all those who may need it, will identify all strategic and operational risks, provide assessment and record the measures in place to manage those risks.
- Performance of risk management activities will be measured against the Company's aims and objectives.
- An understanding of risk and its management will be built up at all levels in the organisation, with partners and key stakeholders, combined with consistent treatment of risk across the organisation.

RISK ASSESSMENT

Risk management involves four key stages, known as the 'Risk Management Cycle':

1   Identification of each risk.
2   Evaluation of each risk.
3   Control of each risk.
4   Monitoring.

RISK IDENTIFICATION

This involves identifying the risks to which the Company is exposed. Risk can be categorised in many ways but the following *seven* categories are the most commonly used.

Strategic risks
The risks that impact the medium and long-term goals and objectives of the organisation. Managing strategic risks often is a responsibility of the Risk Management Committee (RMC). Such risks include:

- Political: Failure to deliver government policy.
- Economic: Implications of changes to the Economy (for example inflation, interest rates and so on).
- Social: Failing to respond to the effects of changes in demographic, residential or socio-economic trends or to reflect these in the company's objectives.
- Customer: Failure to meet the current and changing needs of customers

Operational risks
These are the risks that managers and staff will encounter in the daily course of work.

- Competitive: Failure to deliver value for money, product quality, and so on.
- Physical: Hazards relating to fire, security, accident prevention, health and safety (for example, buildings, vehicles, plant and equipment).
- Contractual: Failure of contractors to deliver services or products to time, cost and specification.

Financial risks

Failures in financial planning, budgetary control, funding shortfall or mismanagement and inaccurate or inadequate monitoring and reporting,

Reputational risks

Those associated with media coverage and any action or inaction that can damage the Company's good name.

IT and information risks

- Technological: Lack of capacity to deal with the pace and scale of change, or of ability to use technology to address changing demands. Also may include the consequences of internal technological failures.
- Physical IT: Equipment failures such as IT, telephony, machinery, and so on.

Regulatory risks

- Legislative: Not responding, or acting contrary to, either national or international legislation.
- Environmental: Failing to adequately assess the environmental consequences of the Company actions (for example, energy efficiency, pollution, recycling, emissions, land use, and so on).
- Legal: Failures related to breaches of legislation.

People risks

- Professional: Failures such as lack of financial acumen, inattention to the welfare of tenants, lack of consultation on developments, and so on.
- Staff and management: Loss of key personnel or the inability to retain them.

Evaluation

There are many tools that can be used to help identify potential risks:

- workshops
- scenario planning
- analysing past claims and other losses
- analysing past corporate incidents/failures
- health and safety inspections
- induction training
- performance review and development interviews
- staff and customer feedback.

Having identified areas of potential risk, they need to be analysed by:

- an assessment of impact
- an assessment of likelihood.

This can be done by recording the results using the risk matrix in Figure 2.1.

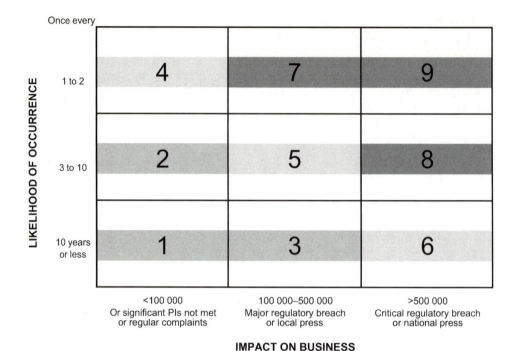

Figure 2.1   Risk assessment matrix

EXPLANATION OF MATRIX

Scores of 1–9

The scores indicate relative risk: 9 being the greatest overall risk, 8 the next and so on. A critical impact with a high likelihood will score 9, while a critical impact with a low likelihood will score 6. A significant impact with a medium likelihood will score 5, whilst a low impact with a high likelihood will score 4.

Impact on the business

The descriptors for each column and row are simply examples and will need to be set specifically by the organisation by taking into account its types of risk and their relative likelihood of occurrence. Examples of impact may be the following:

- High – will have a catastrophic effect on the operation. May result in either:
  - major financial loss (more than 5 per cent of total costs or revenue);
  - major service disruption (+ five days);
  - death of an individual or several people;
  - complete failure of project or extreme delay (over two months);
  - adverse publicity in national press.
- Medium – will have a significant but not catastrophic effect on the operation. May result in either:
  - significant financial loss (more than 2 per cent of total costs or revenue);
  - significant business disruption (two to five days);
  - severe injury to an individual or several people;

– adverse effect on project or significant slippage;
– adverse publicity in regional press.
- Low – where the consequences will not be as severe and any associated losses and or financial implications will be relatively low:
  – some effect on service delivery (one day);
  – minor injury to an individual or several people;
  – a few customers complain.

Likelihood

- High – very likely to happen (within one to two years).
- Medium – likely to happen less frequently and is more difficult to predict (likely to happen once every three to ten years.
- Low – most unlikely to happen (once every ten years or less frequently).

MITIGATION

Using the risk matrix produces a risk-rating score which will enable risks to be prioritised using one or more of the four Ts:

Tolerate	accept the risk
Treat	take cost effective actions to reduce the risk
Transfer	let someone else take the risk (for example, by insurance or passing responsibility for the risk to a contractor)
Terminate	agree that the risk is too high and do not proceed with the project or activity

Risk assessment and risk matrices provide a powerful and easy to use tool for the identification, assessment and control of business risk. It enables managers to consider the whole range of categories of risk affecting a business activity. The technique can assist in the prioritisation of risks and decisions on allocation of resources. Decisions can then be made concerning the adequacy of existing control measures and the need for further action. It can be directed at the business activity as a whole or on individual departments/sections/functions or indeed projects.

MONITORING

Effective risk management requires a reporting and review structure to ensure that risks are effectively identified and assessed and that appropriate controls and responses are in place. Regular audits should be carried out and performance standards reviewed to identify opportunities for improvement. Changes in the business and the environment in which it operates must be identified and appropriate modifications made to systems.

The monitoring process should provide assurance that there are appropriate controls in place and that the procedures are understood and followed.

Having carried out a risk assessment, managers must:

- ensure that the agreed control measures continue to be applied;

- check whether there have been any changes in circumstances that necessitate a fresh risk assessment being carried out;
- formally review all risk assessments affecting their areas of activity at least annually as part of the management planning process.

Reporting lines and accountabilities for risk management are set out in the following section.

STEPS IN RISK ASSESSMENT

- Identify the business activity/function/project the assessment is to be focused on.
- Specify the business objective.
- Identify the threats to the objective.
- Identify the likelihood and severity of the impact of the risk on the business objective.
- Plot the risk score on the risk matrix.
- Identify the risk control measures.
- Reassess the level of residual risk after control measures are listed and re-plot residual risk on the risk matrix. This will give a measure of the effectiveness of the various control measures and help raise awareness of their importance.

The residual score should be at a level that is acceptable to management. The risk assessment process involves all managers and should be repeated at least annually (more frequently if there are changed circumstances) to monitor the effectiveness of the risk control measures implemented.

Risk assessments are relatively easy to do and will provide us with an overall and graphic view of the risks we face and which are affecting the business activity. By doing so we will be better placed to rely on the strategic and operational decisions taken by the organisation.

RISK REGISTER

The organisation will maintain a register of all significant risks that may affect our ability to achieve our objectives and the control measures in place for dealing with them. New risks identified through the decision-making process should be notified for inclusion in the register. Risk Management Committee members and managers must review the adequacy and appropriateness of the entries in the risk register whenever circumstances change and in any event not less than annually as part of the service planning process.

DECISION MAKING AND PROJECT PLANNING

The Company needs to be able to demonstrate that it took reasonable steps to consider the risks involved in a decision. Risk therefore needs to be addressed at the point at which decisions are being taken. Where the Board and the RMC are being asked to make decisions they should be advised of the risks associated with the recommendations being made.

Risk management is also an integral part of project management, both in terms of the initial project/solution design and as part of ensuring that projects are delivered successfully.

Where the Company provides services in partnership with others or through a contractor, potential risks that could prevent success still need to be considered just as though we were providing those services ourselves. Whilst these risks may be managed through formal contracts and partnership agreements that clearly allocate risks to the appropriate parties, failure by either or any one of those parties to manage their risks effectively can have serious consequences for the other.

Before entering into partnership, joint working or business contract arrangements, the prospective partners and contractors should be asked to provide evidence of their approach to risk management.

The following documents will in future include formal risk assessments:

- all reports to RMC;
- business cases and project plans;
- recommendations to the Board;
- management plans – where these include proposals for additional areas of activity, to cease particular activities or change the way in which any activities are undertaken.

Where managers take decisions or review procedures under delegated powers they should similarly undertake a risk assessment prior to making a decision and retain a record of this for future use.

ACCOUNTABILITIES, ROLES AND RESPONSIBILITIES

An appropriate Director should take overall responsibility for developing the organisation's approach to risk management. Responsibility for the day-to-day management of specific risks lies with the managers and staff, as they are the people directly responsible for different business activities.

The different roles and responsibilities for risk management are shown in Table 2.1:

Table 2.1 Roles and responsibilities for risk management

Group	Role
The Board	• To formally approve the Company's Risk Management Strategy • Consider risk as part of all decisions • Review annually the Company's arrangements for risk management
Risk Management Committee	• Ensure the Company manages risk effectively through the Risk Management Strategy and report to Board annually • Identify strategic risks affecting the organisation and make recommendations to the Board as to the ways in which these will be managed
Managers	• Ensure risk is managed effectively in each function within the agreed strategy and report to RMC quarterly • Identify individual risks affecting their activities,

ensure that these are recorded in the risk register
and that appropriate control measures are in place for
managing those risks

- Continually monitor the adequacy and effectiveness
  of all control measures and report to their RMC
  member
- Formally review all arrangements for risk
  management affecting their activity at least annually
  as part of business planning

All employees

- Undertake their job within risk management
  guidelines including compliance with all control
  measures that have been identified
- Report hazards/risks to their managers

Internal Audit

- Monitor and review whether risks have been
  adequately identified and included in the risk
  register
- Monitor the adequacy and effectiveness of the control
  measures in place
- Make recommendations to managers, RMC and the
  Board as necessary

MONITORING SUCCESS

The Company will monitor the impact of risk management activities and the success of the
risk management strategy using the following criteria (Table 2.2):

Table 2.2   Monitoring the impact of risk management activities and the success of risk management
strategies

Issue	Indicator	Comment
Integration of RM into culture of the organisation and raising awareness of RM	• Staff recognising their role and responsibility for RM in their area • Number of reports for decision that demonstrate risk assessment • Responses to audit and inspection	• By audit of reports and documentary evidence of decisions • By audit of responses
Enabling change	• Post-event assessment – how we managed major changes and other projects	
Minimisation of losses, injury and inconvenience	• Number and length of disruption to production • Level of complaints, claims and so on • Levels of write offs	• Measure response and recovery performance as well as frequency • Informed by existing strategies and processes

Introduce risk management framework	• Feedback from staff • Compliance with standards	
Minimising cost of risk	• Annual insurance premiums • Level of reserves • Uninsured losses • Management and project costs	• Will incorporate budget and capital project overspends, fraud, write offs, claims, premiums and so on

Introducing a risk management programme

The following describes the suggested approach and methodology for introducing an embedded risk management process. The programme should be modelled on and measured against the worldwide best practice and international risk management standards referred to earlier.

STAGE 1 PLANNING

- finalisation of assignment brief with relevant Director, with input from and agreement of Risk Management Steering Group;
- preparation of timetable in consultation with key personnel;
- meetings with Chief Executive, Deputy Chief Executive, Director of Finance and Chairman of the Risk Management Steering Committee to get their perspectives and outline the process;
- establishment of specific milestone dates;
- agreement of contacts, specific format of workshops and attendees;
- establishment of workshop dates and so on;
- determination of reporting mechanisms.

STAGE 2 RAISING MANAGEMENT AWARENESS

- setting the context for risk management;
- imagine any of the following newspaper headlines:
    Group Pay Through the Nose for Ailing Company
    Executives of Acquired Business Sue for Compensation
    Company Fined €10m for Failing to Follow Environmental Regulations
    Major Fraud Uncovered
    Millions Wasted as IT Project Fails
    Number of Complaints Against Company Rockets
    Bank Collapse – Organisation Loses €15m
    Supplier Payments Duplicated Due to System Error
- sector developments and the resultant challenges;
- key requirements – critical dates;
- wrong assumptions about risk – why risk and insurance are not synonymous;
- definitions and outline of Aus/NZ Risk Management Standard – the only internationally recognised risk management standard;
- the link between risk and culture – is the organisation primarily risk averse or risk embracing?

- the implications of changes in risk culture;
- the critical link between strategy and risk;
- benefits of a formal approach to risk management;
- explanation of the risk workshop process;
- outline of current procedures and policies relating to risk management;
- identification of risk (including interactive session);
- categories of risk;
- risk mitigation, risk exposures and identification of opportunities;
- risk matrices and risk registers;
- the need to embed the risk process.

STAGE 3 STRATEGIC RISK ASSESSMENT WORKSHOP

Risk identification: The introduction of a consistent and tailored model for risk identification needs to be established. A matrix to assist in the assessment of the materiality of likelihood and potential impact will also be produced. These will be tailored to specific limits and exposures relevant to the organisation. Risk categories will be assessed and finalised to ensure consistency of reporting and tracking the key risks. The above will all be established through discussions prior to the workshop.

Workshop outline

- brief explanation of the workshop, its objectives and deliverables;
- ground rules;
- discussion and agreement of strategic objectives;
- thought provokers and diagnostic questions – to encourage the participants to consider the critical risks;
- facilitated risk identification (individually by Post-it® notes);
- explanation of risk categories to be used;
- sifting and clustering the risks by means of the risk categories;
- measuring the risks (impact and likelihood of occurrence);
- discussion and agreement of significance;
- recording the risks by means of a risk matrix;
- discussion of next steps re output;
- discussion of attendees at risk mitigation workshop.

It is strongly recommended that a separate workshop be held to examine risk mitigation, as it is unlikely that the management team will have enough knowledge of the current procedures to make this element of the process practical. A second half-day workshop a week or so after the initial workshop bringing in the next level of management would be the optimum solution

STAGE 4 STRATEGIC RISK MITIGATION WORKSHOP

- brief review of output from first workshop – first columns of risk register;
- explanation of mitigation workshop and output (completed risk register);
- small focused teams discuss and record mitigation for each risk;
- teams present to full workshop group;

- discussion and agreement of exposures (and opportunities, for example, over managed risks);
- residual risks determined and recorded (via risk matrix);
- action plans debated and owners allocated;
- all columns of risk register completed.

RISK REGISTER

The risk register in the format already determined will be produced. The risk appetite should also be determined together with any risk limits in place.

RISK EXPOSURES

After considering the cost effectiveness and availability of the options for mitigating the risks there will still be residual exposures. It is important to recognise such exposures and to specifically accept them – this is proactive risk management. The consultants will assist the risk owners to evaluate any exposures.

STAGE 5 RISK TRACKING

Having identified the key risks it is important that the process becomes embedded in the organisation. A mechanism therefore is needed to track movements in those risks. To this end a set of Key Risk Indicators (KRI) will be identified. For each KRI a standard level of performance will also be agreed, through discussion, against which actual performance can be measured. Wherever possible this data will be drawn from existing management information. The analysis of this data, together with other risk information that might be identified, will enable regular reports to be designed to show how the risks are changing. The generation of this information will promote an awareness of changes in risks, provide risk management information and, by focusing management attention, prioritise and support the risk management process.

STAGE 6 OPERATIONAL RISK WORKSHOPS

The number of workshops will depend on the complexity and diversity of the organisation. A good guide is to hold workshops with executives who are the direct reports to the Board members and then the managers reporting to those executives, that is, two management layers beneath the Board.

Risk identification workshop outline

A similar process as for the strategic workshops apart from:

- overview of process and outputs (including input to key organisational risks);
- discussion and agreement of operational rather than strategic objectives;
- facilitated risk identification (individually by Post-it® notes). Wider risks will be separated and collated from each workshop and reported upwards.

Risk mitigation workshop outline

A very similar process as for the strategic workshops.

These risks will be grouped together under the generic categories, developed as part of the model in Stage 2, to help ensure that the reporting of risks and their movement is consistent across all activities. From the results achieved it will be possible for managers and specialist staff to assess and consider the actions that they can take to mitigate their business risks at this lower level. The results of the specific reviews can then be escalated into a corporate analysis to identify their potential impact on the organisation's key risks.

By being aware of changes in the risk profile within their parts of the organisation, managers will be able to respond by adopting and adapting their risk management activities. Positive and proactive risk management will be evidenced by improving or deleting redundant or overly costly controls, enhancing the value gained from insurance spending and other contracts or partnerships and through a clearer understanding of the exposures faced.

This consideration of risk forms the basis of Control Risk Self Assessment (CRSA). This technique will provide an organisation with a wide view of risk management that can then be collated and reported. CRSA provides valuable on-going reinforcement to the independent reviews undertaken by Internal Audit, which inevitably will have to be snapshots at a given period of time. Only CRSA can provide a commentary on how risks were actually managed and how thoroughly internal controls operated throughout the whole of the period of account. Such a system would provide an invaluable aid to the continued development of the overall corporate governance and risk management processes.

CRSA does, however, require those with such responsibilities to view these activities positively and to have received sufficient training and support. Careful communication of the benefits is therefore required and could be provided within the assistance given during the assignment.

STAGE 7 CONSOLIDATION AND REPORTING

- collation of output;
- identification of organisation-wide risks not already captured;
- evaluation of such risks and mitigation;
- preparation of summary reports for management team and Risk Management Committee;
- preparation of key risk matrix;
- evaluation of benefits and preparation of success measures;
- determination of optimum approach for sharing output and publicising benefits – including responsibility for action plan follow up;
- development of approach for risk-based decision making using the risk matrices.

Benefits and success measures

The following schedule provides much of the ammunition needed to sell the benefits of a formalised risk management programme and measure its success. Whilst many may appear obvious, management will often fail to recognise many of the positive aspects of risk management. The schedule can therefore be used as a 'pick and mix' menu.

Benefits

Enhances reputation
More innovation
Better strategic awareness
More consistent approach
Focus more on the big picture
Enforces ownership
Less adverse media coverage
Influence change
Help change culture
More informed decisions
Greater comfort to senior management
Facilitates better business planning
Facilitates sensitivity analysis
Encourages thinking out of the box
Better corporate awareness
Better information transfer
Better information for Chief Executive
Enforces risk ownership
Spot the banana skins
Avoid embarrassing systems failures
Enhances understanding of vulnerabilities
Increase chances of objectives being achieved
Identify the key risks and opportunities
Formal documentation of risks
Managing financial risk better
Share knowledge of controls
Identify gaps
Challenge processes
Challenge the status quo
Understand others' roles better
Framework to take calculated risks
More satisfied staff
Encourages people to think
More effective use of resources
Improve accountability
Enhance communication
Break down silos
More informed decision making
More proactive outlook
More confidence
Breeds more openness
Forces prioritisation of resource usage
Improve employee motivation
Manage complaints better
Learn from mistakes

Break down barriers
Better co-ordination
Reduce duplication
Reduce scrutiny
Best value compliance
Tick in the box
Helps Internal Audit profile
Compliance with governance agenda
Improved probity
Enhance asset protection
Regular review and monitoring
Demonstrate delivery to external bodies
Potential lighter touch from external regime
Enhanced assurance
Improve service delivery
Better project planning
Reduce surprises
Release funding to front line services
Better business continuity planning
Minimise assurance costs

Results/Measures

Less waste
Savings – insurance
Reduce claims and other costs
Reduce external audit costs
Projects delivered on time to cost
Reduce complaints
Reduce staff turnover
Less absenteeism
Fewer rethought decisions
Backing more winners – contracts, and so on
Reduction in cost of risk claims
Reduction in stress
More upper quartile delivery
Annual audit letter positive
Better contract prices, and so on
Better satisfaction surveys
Fewer adverse press articles
Fewer Internal Audit recommendations
Fewer regulatory visits
Risk register kept up to date
Reduction in legal challenges
Increased percentage of objectives achieved
Ombudsman cases – number and outcomes
Corporate Governance statement better substantiated

Better league table position
Reduction in cost of risk – uninsured losses claims, and so on
Reduction in proven complaints – press or Ombudsman
Increased funding
Reduction in absenteeism, and so on
Reduction in fraud
Reduction in risk matrix score
Corporate policies enhanced
Less disasters and surprises
Cost reduction in contingency funds
Reduction in over-managed controls
Positive feedback by external agencies
Adding value across service areas
Higher public satisfaction
Extra funding re partnerships
Favourable external inspection reports
Corporate Governance compliance demonstrated
Risk reduction for critical risks
Consistent risk assessment methodology
Best value target delivery
Better member accountability
Better project management

Risk examples

Many different types of risk will be encountered. Table 2.3 provides a checklist of the most common and can be used as a cross reference to risk registers to ensure no categories have been missed.

Table 2.3 Types of risk

	Asset integrity	
Breakdown	Maintenance	Infrastructure failure
Fire	Leaks and spills	Explosion
Security	Shortages of property or material	Safety failures
Asset damage		Sabotage
	Change	
Unable to keep up with pace	Magnitude	Competing initiatives
Poor prioritisation	Focus	Lack of follow through

Competition

Market position change	Number of competitors	Mergers
	Joint ventures	
	Competitor performance and reputation	

Confusion

Mixed signals	Conflicting objectives	Internal politics
Lack of alignment		Power struggles

Contracts

Agreements	Projects	Limits
Restrictions	Lack of responsibility	Ownership
Poor accountability	Unknown liability	Lack of clarity

Country risks

Devaluation	Change of power	Lack of legal compliance
Community disturbance	Instability	Damaging attitudes
Terrorism	Business interruption	Civil unrest
Political crisis	Deregulation	Currency restriction
Infrastructure collapse	Interest rate shifts	Sabotage
Crime	Strikes	Corruption
Regulation	Transparency	Unplanned growth

Customers

Lack of focus	Poor value proposition	Poor identification
Satisfaction	Feedback	Responsiveness
Internal/external	Retention	Pricing

Financial

Price	Trading	Interest rates
New financial products	Taxation	Currency
Invoicing	Availability of capital costs	Liquidity
		Financial reporting
Counterparty		
	Debt/equity position	
Cash flows		

Fraud

Defalcation	Bribery	Embezzlement
Misrepresentation	Theft	Organised crime
Blackmail	Illegal acts	Unauthorised use
Falsification		Data hacking

Group interaction

Alignment	Conflict of interests	Transfer pricing
Internal competition	Duplication	Co-ordination

Portfolio valuation and management

Health & Safety

Equipment failure	Environmental impact	Death
Personal injury	Illness	Disease
Pollution	Property damage	Contamination
Emission	Noise	Regulatory non-compliance
Litigation	Substance abuse	Catastrophic event

Information

Integrity	Accuracy	Security
Reliability	Timeliness	Retention
Usability	Computer virus	Accessibility
Data overload	Misuse	Infrastructure

Knowledge

Learning from mistakes	Copyrights	Patents
Trademarks		Corporate memory
Intellectual property	Hidden or false assumptions	Knowledge sharing
Staff departures	Reinvention of the wheel	Deception

Management

Style	Tone	Acceptance
Attitudes to risk and control	Competence	Judgement
Experience		Vision
Consistency	Direction	Decision making
Failure	Communication	Flexibility
Performance measurement		Ability to adapt

Markets

Competition	Market share	Substitutes
Obsolescence	New products	Product life cycle
Margins	Pricing regulations	Liberalisation
Quality	Demand	Long-term contracts
Volatility	Supply availability	Access
	Profitability	

Natural events

Earthquake	Flood	Fire
Storm	Global warming	Noise
Contamination	Pollution	Climate change

Operational

Cost management	Efficiency	Capacity
Reliability	Unplanned shutdown	Continuity
Measurement	Product quality	Logistics
	Supply	Cycle time
Distribution	Inventory management	Technology
Information	Interfaces	Design failure
Pricing	Marketing	Interruption

Organisation

Corporate Governance	Structure	Complexity
Outsourcing	Core competencies	Decision making
Changes	Interfaces	Concentration of power
Working environment	Culture	Boundaries

People

Communications	Direction	Trust
Human error	Performance and reward systems	Work load
Morale	Expertise	Challenge
Stress	Attraction and retention	
Loyalty	of key skills	
	Experience	Conflicts of interest
Competence	Improper relationships	Leadership
Resistance to change	Employee value proposition	Pricing
Turnover	Flexibility	Re-training

Reputation

Liabilities	Brand integrity	Competition law
Public perception	Relationships with shareholders	Transparency
Market ratings	Financial market perceptions	Trademarks
Product failure	Infringement	

Stakeholders and partners

Strength of relationships	Ability to influence	Competing interest
Conflict of interest	Shifting or hidden agendas	Different perceptions
Ignorance	Defective advice	Joint ventures
Business principles		Failure of partner

Strategy and decision making

Opportunities	Strengths	Acquisitions
Threats	Market entry or exit	Portfolio management
Valuation	Key assumptions	Business models
Divestments	Investment evaluation	Planning
Doing nothing	Innovation	Lack of foresight

Systems

Compatibility	Integration	Interfaces
Selection	Contingencies	Design
Stability	Implementation	Security
Flexibility	Infrastructure	Usability

Technology

	Growth of e-commerce/m-commerce	
Innovation	Identity/group opportunities	
Product development	Alternatives	Research
Access to new technologies	Industry shift	Obsolescence

The Australia/New Zealand Risk Management Standard 4360

There are a number of risk management standards in the world but the Australia/New Zealand Risk Standard is the only one that is internationally recognised, that is, it is used across the world. You can get a copy of the standard via the Australian Standards Institute website, www.standards.com.au, and the standard number is 4360:2004. The cost for downloading the standard and the excellent accompanying guideline is US$65 (in early 2005). Alternatively you can order a hard copy (which costs a little more).

This standard which was conceived in 1995 and has had two revisions (1999 and 2004) is widely regarded as the skeleton for modern risk management. The standard was developed using the COSO* guidelines which were published in 1992 and have been adopted as the generally recognised standard for Corporate Governance. (NB The Canadians also produced guidelines – known as Co Co – which are also well regarded in this field.)

The current version of the standard (2004) builds on the earlier research and incorporates greater emphasis on the importance of embedding risk management practices into the organisation's culture than the 1999 Standard and increased emphasis on the

---

*COSO = Committee of Sponsoring Organisations (of the Treadway Commission) – established in the USA to develop standards of Governance and Internal Control.

positive aspect of risk management. The essence of the standard is to expound a simple repeatable process for evaluating, measuring and controlling risks.

The COSO Framework for Enterprise Risk Management

Equally, in 2004, COSO produced an excellent set of guidance notes entitled *Enterprise Risk Management – Integrated Framework*. This provides a benchmark for organisations to help evaluate the effectiveness of their approach to risk management across the organisation. This, with its companion document, *Application Techniques*, provides a very comprehensive explanation of Enterprise Risk Management (ERM). The framework can be downloaded from www.COSO.org for about US$75 (at the time of writing).

THE FRAMEWORK

The Committee of Sponsoring Organisations of the Treadway Commission is represented by five professional bodies, namely:

- The Institute of Internal Auditors
- American Institute of Certified Public Accountants
- American Accounting Association
- Institute of Management Accountants in the USA
- Financial Executives Institute of the USA.

The published goal of COSO is to improve the quality of financial reporting through a focus on Corporate Governance, ethical practices and internal control.

DEFINITION OF INTERNAL CONTROL

The COSO definition, as you will see, links very neatly with the earlier risk definitions:

A process effected by an entity's board of directors, management and other personnel, designed to provide reasonable assurance regarding the achievement of objectives.

The COSO framework identifies five components of Internal Control:

1 The Control Environment
2 Risk Assessment
3 Control Activities
4 Information and Communication
5 Monetary

Each of the elements of the framework is crucial to the Internal Audit process.

In addition to the issues regarding risk assessment already discussed in this chapter, the framework poses a number of questions which need to be asked by Internal Audit as part of their review of Corporate Governance and Assurance.

Ethics

- Do the Board and Senior Management lead by example by establishing and practising the highest level of integrity and ethical behaviour?
- Is there a written code of conduct for employees which is reinforced by training and requirements for annual written statements of compliance by senior level personnel?
- Are performance and incentive targets set realistically or do they create unhealthy pressure or too much focus on achievement of short-term results (to the detriment of the long-term aspirations and goals)?
- Is there a clear fraud prevention policy in place and do all employees recognise that fraudulent activities at any level within the organisation will not be tolerated?
- Are ethics and ethical standards incorporated into the criteria for evaluation of individual and business performance?
- Does management react in an appropriate manner when being given bad news by business functions?

Risk and internal control

- Are risks and exposures discussed openly with the Board of Directors?
- Is relevant reliable internal and external information or risk and controls available to senior management in a timely manner?
- Do management demonstrate that they take responsibility and accountability for the risks and controls under their area of responsibility?
- Is the operation of controls mutually monitored by management?
- Are clear responsibilities assigned for this monetary process?
- Are appropriate criteria established to assess and evaluate the effectiveness of controls?
- Are opportunities to enhance controls implemented on a timely basis?

INTERNAL AUDIT

You may need to have a peer review or benchmarking exercise to answer the following questions but these are certainly thought provokers:

- Does Internal Audit have the support of top management and the Board of Directors as a whole?
- Are the organisational relationship and reporting lines between Internal Audit and senior executives appropriate?
- Does Internal Audit have open access (privately if necessary) to all senior management and the chairman of the Audit Committee?
- Do key audit personnel have the necessary level of expertise?

The COSO framework is intended to challenge management and auditors and provides a very good reference document for all Internal Audit functions.

The Sarbanes-Oxley Act 2002

The Sarbanes-Oxley Act in the United States, implemented following the Enron and WorldCom scandals, has also sought to focus much more attention on risk management and it is now quoted on the US stock exchange to the extent that the CEO and CFO both now have to sign off control statements at the end of each year.

The Act prescribes a system of federal oversight of Public Auditors through a Public Company Oversight Board, a new set of auditor independence rules, new disclosure requirements and harsh penalties for persons who are responsible for accounting or reporting violations.

For most organisations, the Act's most noticeable impact is in the area of Corporate Governance. The Act will force many companies to adopt significant changes in their internal controls and the roles played by audit committees and senior management in the financial reporting process.

Most significantly, the Act imposes new responsibilities on Chief Executives and CFOs and exposes them to much greater potential liability.

Under the Act, audit committees are subject to heightened independence standards, including prohibition of non-independent members. Companies are required to grant the audit committee specific levels of controls over the relationship with its auditors, including exclusive hiring, firing and spending authority. Audit committees are also required to establish rules for the treatment of complaints regarding internal controls or accounting issues, as well as confidential submission by employees of concerns regarding questionable accounting or auditing matters.

The Act also stipulates that periodic reports must include disclosures regarding internal controls, non-audit services provided by the External Auditor and material from balance sheet transactions. These reports must also disclose whether the Company has adopted a code of ethics for senior financial officers, and if not, why not.

IMPLICATIONS FOR INTERNAL AUDIT

Management must publicly state its responsibility for internal control and provide an assessment of the effectiveness of the internal control structure. Internal Audit will play an important role in providing such assurance to management.

The Directors and financial executives will be required to certify in each annual and semi-annual report that they are responsible for establishing and maintaining internal controls, just as they are under the UK Combined Code requirements.

They also need to certify that the internal controls have been designed to ensure that material information relating to the organisation is made known to them, and that they have evaluated the effectiveness of such controls within 90 days prior to the report.

They also have to disclose to the External Auditors and the Audit Committee all significant deficiencies in the design or operation of internal controls and any fraud, whether or not this is material. Again management will be relying heavily upon Internal Audit to give them appropriate assurance.

External Audit have to attest to and report on management's assertions regarding internal control and the Head of Internal Audit will be required to assure management that the systems and processes are operating as planned.

Other standards

There are other useful standards that have been developed and produced in the last few years. The IRM (Institute of Risk Management in the UK) issued, in 2002, with ALARM (Association of Local Authority Risk Managers in the UK), a standard and this provides useful guidance, particularly an excellent risk glossary. This can be downloaded for free from the IRM's website (www.theirm.org).

Another very important standard which is specific to the financial services sector but well worth reference for organisations in other sectors, is the Basel reports. Basel I was published in 2000 and its successor, Basel II in 2003, the latter of which seeks to tie in risk management to the cost of capital and has generated a great deal of argument and debate amongst the financial services community. Useful reference material on Basel II can be found on www.bis.org, 'the Implementation of Basel II – Practical Considerations'. The book entitled *The Basel II Rating* by Marc Lambrecht and published by Gower provides a full explanation of the standard.

It is very important that the Internal Audit functions familiarise themselves fully with the relevant risk standards, particularly as they will almost certainly be required to give the Board their annual evaluation of the effectiveness of the processes in place to identify, mitigate and control the key risks impacting the organisation. Auditing the risk management process is a key facet of the modern Internal Audit role and is explained in some depth in a series of position statements issued by the Institute of Internal Auditors, culminating in the latest 'The Role of Internal Audit in Enterprise-wide Risk Management' – www.iia.org.uk.

This position statement confirms that the core role of Internal Audit is to provide objective assurance to the Board on the effectiveness of risk management. Indeed research entitled 'The Value Agenda' produced by the Institute of Internal Auditors – UK and Ireland – and Deloitte and Touche in 2003 has shown that Board Directors and Internal Auditors agree that the two most important ways that Internal Audit provides value to the organisation are in providing objective assurance that the major business risks are being managed appropriately and providing assurance that the risk management and internal control framework are operating effectively.

3 Refocusing the Audit Role to Embrace Risk

The changing scope of modern Internal Audit

As highlighted in Chapter 1, the Internal Audit role is changing rapidly. The broader assurance role required by management and the opportunity to be involved in assessing the effectiveness of governance and risk management are both exciting and challenging developments. The opportunity to carry out a more consultancy-type role and the continuing need to add measurable value all contribute to the interest and complexity of the role. But how far should Internal Audit go? What are the options available to the function?

Understanding the expectations of Chief Executives

In mid-2000, I completed a piece of research to determine the expectations of Financial Directors in the FTSE 250 companies towards Internal Audit and its future. This research was repeated in mid-2002 and again in 2004.

Whilst the FTSE 250 list has changed during the four-year period with mergers, acquisitions and changes in organisations' fortunes, the research remains valid – as it is seeking qualitative judgements regarding a common function.

Forty-seven per cent of companies responded to the 2000 survey. This percentage increased to 63 per cent in the 2002 survey and 65 per cent in the latest research – making the results statistically significant.

The results from a risk management and governance viewpoint were very revealing.

OBJECTIVES OF THE RESEARCH

To determine from the Director responsible for Internal Audit

- the current perception of the role and value added by Internal Audit in their organisations;
- what the function needs to do to enhance this perception;
- what the main focus of Internal Audit is currently and whether this was the same as predicted two years ago;
- how the value delivered by the function is assessed;
- the main challenges that IA need to overcome to meet the expectations;
- the implications of the Corporate Governance requirements on the Internal Audit relationship.

During the research other key data was obtained

- how many companies responding have an Internal Audit function;
- what proportion of these functions are wholly or partially outsourced;
- the extent to which functions have changed in size during the last two years;
- information on how the function is marketed;
- the extent of the Internal Audit/External Audit relationship.

THE INTERNAL AUDIT REPORTING LINE

In view of the expected changes to the Internal Audit reporting relationship heralded by the 2000 research, it was decided to widen the research from just the Financial Director's perception (as in the 2000 survey) to encompass the Director with responsibility for the function, whomever that was.

The following question was therefore asked: To whom does the Head of Internal Audit report? The response is shown in Figure 3.1 (a–c)

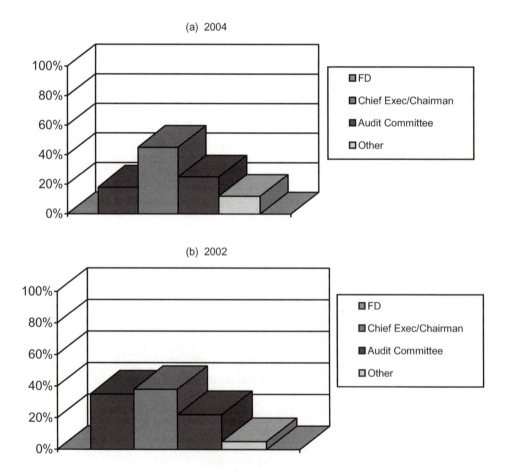

(a) 2004

(b) 2002

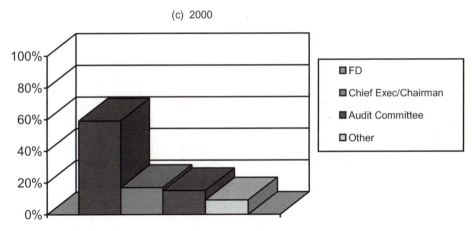

Figure 3.1   To whom does the Head of Internal Audit report?
(a) 2004 survey responses; (b) 2002 survey responses;
(c) 2000 survey responses.

A major shift in the reporting line has occurred in the four-year period.

In 2000, 59 per cent of Internal Audit functions reported to the Financial Director. This has reduced to 18 per cent in 2004. The survey revealed that the most common direct reporting relationship is now to the Chief Executive (this has more than doubled from 17 per cent to 45 per cent in the four years).

Asked what the main thrust of the function was in 2002 and how this would change in 2004, the following picture emerged. The actual situation in 2004 is even more pronounced than predicted two years ago (Table 3.1).

Table 3.1   The main thrust of the Internal Audit function

	2002	Predicted 2004	Actual 2004
	Percentage	Percentage	Percentage
Business risk orientated	72	85	89
Financial systems based	7	3	1
Operational systems based	10	3	2
Compliance orientated	6	2	1
Internal consultancy	1	2	1
Value for money	2	1	0
Corporate Governance	2	4	6

The trend towards business risk orientation, as the principal thrust of the function, has continued with a vengeance with the financial systems and compliance focus reducing even faster than expected a couple of years ago.

The other noticeable trend, and not one predicted when the survey was completed in 2000 was the emergence of Corporate Governance as an important focus. This clearly recognises the significant role taken by many Internal Audit functions in leading or facilitating the Corporate Governance programme. More than half the organisations reported that their Internal Audit function had taken a leading role in governance evaluation and reporting.

In 2002 less than half the organisations responding expected that the current focus of their IA function would be the same in 2004. In fact the change turned out to be even more dramatic with 65 per cent of functions having made a change in their primary focus (mainly towards business risk).

The trend predicted in 2002, namely companies which then still had a compliance orientation for their IA function, expecting this to move to an operational approach (but not to a business risk orientation), was not borne out in practice as most did indeed move directly to a business risk approach.

CORPORATE GOVERNANCE

The following questions were asked about corporate governance in the 2004 survey:

- Does your company use CRSA as part of the Corporate Governance process?
  YES   =   93 per cent
- What level of involvement does the Internal Audit function have in the Corporate Governance process?

Leading the programme (on management's behalf)	=	9 per cent
Evaluating the process and reporting to management	=	19 per cent
Facilitating the business risk programme	=	43 per cent
Support role, for example, attending workshops, and so on	=	24 per cent
Minimal involvement	=	5 per cent

Internal Audit departments have therefore forged a strong role for themselves in the Corporate Governance arena, which is certainly good news for the credibility and recognition of the function.

CHIEF EXECUTIVE'S PERCEPTION

1   What perception do you have of Internal Audit?

	2004	2002	2000
	%	%	%
Positive	66	60	45
Luke-warm	22	26	28
Negative	12	14	27

To analyse these responses

POSITIVE RESPONSES (66 PER CENT OF TOTAL)

Specific comments included:

- focused on the most significant risks;
- a transformation in the function under the new Head of Audit;
- professional and powerful to the organisation;
- a great asset to the business;
- professional function held in high regard by the business;
- excellent assurance provider to the Board;
- changed role well to meet the Corporate Governance challenge;
- makes a significant contribution;
- driver of business risk programme;
- increasingly adding measurable value.

It was disturbing that in these top British companies, four years ago less than half the directors felt really positive about the contribution that their Internal Audit functions were making. This percentage has increased to 66 per cent, but this still means that one out of three departments are failing to meet management's expectations for it.

LUKE-WARM RESPONSES (22 PER CENT OF TOTAL)

Comments included:

- needs to more involved with business issues;
- starting to be more challenging;
- providing a useful if rather basic service;
- competent but needs to raise profile;
- capable department but needs broader mix of skills;
- generally good but needs to add greater value.

LESS COMPLIMENTARY RESPONSES (12 PER CENT OF TOTAL)

Whilst the negative perceptions have reduced significantly from 27 per cent to 12 per cent over the four years, reflecting positive actions taken by some functions to improve practices and value added, there is still cause for concern.
    Specific comments included:

- still too compliance orientated;
- needs to get a much higher profile;
- quality of staff causes concern;
- slow to pick up the Corporate Governance challenges;
- not really integrated into the business;
- not a strategic player;
- poor on delivery;
- not rising to the challenges as much as they should.

The messages emerging are that whilst improvements have been made, and many departments have developed a new role for themselves, there is still much to be done in some organisations.

2   What would the function have to do to enhance your perception of it?

	2004 %	2002 %
Build a higher profile/be more strategic	27	20
Enhance skills/quality of staff	25	26
Become more risk orientated	15	13
Take a broader Corporate Governance role	12	10
Become more business/operationally orientated	8	16
Be more proactive/responsive/innovative	5	9
Measure value added better	8	6

Specific comments were:

- Skills and staff
  - enhance calibre of audit management;
  - introduce a broader range of personnel;
  - use audit as a fast track development route;
  - get more operational knowledge.
- Business/operational orientation
  - become more of a business partner;
  - get involved in the major issues;
  - get more involved in major systems under development.
- Profile/risk orientation
  - deal with the business units at a more strategic level;
  - manage the risk embedding process;
  - provide specific assurance re. Corporate Governance.

THE INTERNAL AUDIT FUNCTION

1   Does your company have an Internal Audit function? (whether in-house or outsourced)

	%
Respondent companies have an established function	98
Respondent companies do not but are considering establishing or re-establishing one	1
Respondent companies do not and are not considering having one	1
Respondents in the 2000 survey had an Internal Audit function	94

2   If you have an Internal Audit function is this in-house or outsourced?

	%
Functions are provided in-house	96
Fully or significantly oursourced	4

Interestingly, the trend to full outsourcing of Internal Audit appears to have been reversed.

In 2000, 7 per cent of functions were fully or significantly outsourced. This has fallen to 4 per cent in 2004. A number of organisations reported bringing previously outsourced functions back in house.

3   *If you have an in-house Internal Audit function do you currently obtain any Internal Audit services or support from an external source?*

	%
Yes	65
No	35

An even higher percentage of organisations source some Internal Audit services externally than they did in 2002 (52 per cent).

In most cases, however, the respondents reported that this is a minor but growing proportion of the total workload.

According to the information provided by respondents, there is a *definite* trend towards outsourcing certain Internal Audit services.

4   *Which services are outsourced?*

	2004 %	2002 %
Specialist IT audits	25	21
Overseas locations	22	20
To supplement in-house resources	18	16
Ad-hoc special assignments (for example, forensic work and fraud investigation)	15	21
Benchmarking studies	10	6
Treasury	5	8
Integrated auditing	5	8

According to information provided, organisations are finding it more cost effective and efficient to outsource the audits of overseas locations, particularly those where language difficulties would be encountered.

Specialist audits/investigations are also receiving external support, for example, forensic investigations and specialist IT reviews such as Network Security. Internal Audit is also now much more likely to supplement their resources on an ad-hoc basis from outside the company.

The other growth areas are in carrying out benchmarking studies (that is, to benchmark the Internal Audit department against its peers).

Summary

CURRENT PERCEPTION

As can be seen, the Chief Executives' perception of Internal Audit in the FTSE 250 companies responding to the survey was by no means universally positive, although there was a marked improvement in the two years since the last survey.

Still 34 per cent of the companies were either lukewarm or negative about the function and its contribution to the business. The main concerns were that the function had not risen sufficiently to the Corporate Governance challenges or were still guarding their independence – to the detriment of value to the business. Many functions were still lacking in appropriate skills (or had a poor mix of personnel – that is, still too many accountants and not enough professionals from other disciplines).

Even many of the companies who were positive about their Internal Audit function cited the above issues as areas for improvement.

WHAT NEEDS TO BE DONE?

There was a significant measure of agreement by the Directors responsible for Internal Audit on what needs to be done to improve the contribution of Internal Audit (and consequently their perception of it).

The six main recommendations were virtually the same as in 2002:

1   Enhance skills within the function and the quality of the staff.
2   Become much more business risk orientated.
3   Build a higher profile by linking in more directly to the organisation's strategic objectives.
4   Take a broader Corporate Governance role.
5   Measure the value added by the function more effectively.
6   Become more of a business partner.

FOCUS OF INTERNAL AUDIT

There was a direct correlation between the key focus or main thrust of the Internal Audit function and the positive (or otherwise) perception.

Those companies who reported that the main thrust of their Internal Audit was business risk based (85 per cent of the respondents) were also those who regarded the function more positively.

The significance of this trend is also reflected in the fact that Directors expected that business risk orientation, as the main thrust of the department, would rise from 72 per cent to 85 per cent by the year 2004, but in fact the actual figure was even higher (89 per cent).

MAIN CHALLENGES FOR INTERNAL AUDIT

The main challenges (in addition to broadening the skill base and extending the scope of the work programme to encompass all key business risks) were to enhance the cost effectiveness and value added by the function.

A further challenge was to gain greater acceptance from senior management and thereby be in a position to influence strategic thinking. This in turn should enhance the reputation of the function and provide the opportunity for Internal Audit to become a greater source of future management talent for the business.

The final challenge cited by a number of Directors was for Internal Audit to take a broader role in the Corporate Governance agenda.

Options for involvement of Internal Audit in risk management

There are a number of options for Internal Audit in relation to risk management programmes. It is generally considered to be inappropriate that Internal Audit should manage the whole risk management programme, for, if they do, they act as management (which has always been rightly regarded as conflicting with their independence). However, if senior management believe there is no other sufficiently independent function to carry out this role, if, for example, the organisation has not established a specific risk management function, then it is recognised from a pragmatic point of view, that Internal Audit may be able to take on this role. Internal Audit needs to ensure that the Board recognises the potential difficulty with independence which will be caused. Internal Audit certainly cannot credibly audit the risk management process later.

It is much better for Internal Audit not to take the lead role but it is certainly quite acceptable for them to facilitate risk workshops. This creates a very good link because Internal Audit are not then identifying the risks themselves, they are simply facilitating the process by which management identify the risks. It is clearly a very positive approach and one that has been adopted widely. Internal Audit could alternatively jointly facilitate the workshops with a member of management or indeed an external consultant. Many of the workshops that I have facilitated have been carried out in conjunction with Internal Audit. Bearing in mind that an external consultant can only really kick-start the process, it is very important that there is an internal 'owner' to drive the programme forward when the consultant has left. Internal Audit is ideally placed to be able to facilitate.

NB To ensure that senior management recognise the need to take accountability for the risk management process following facilitation support from external consultants a clause should be included in all proposals for risk management consultancy work such as:

> *Throughout the assignment the consultant will work alongside your management. Our aim is to ensure that we transfer our knowledge of embedded risk management to ensure that you can successfully manage the process at the end of the assignment. To this end, and to keep costs to a minimum, it is suggested that a member of staff is nominated to work with the consultant on the assignment. It is therefore assumed that we will work closely with the Head of Internal Audit in this regard.*

If Internal Audit does not facilitate the programme then certainly the very least that they should do is attend the workshops as a participant. Another possible option is to monitor progress of the action plans determined by management to address the risk exposures and exploit opportunities. Even if Internal Audit involvement is very limited they can, and should, still provide a critical role; to compare management's perception of the controls in place to mitigate the risks with the actual controls in place.

It is my view that the more positive a role Internal Audit take in the process the better it is for both the function and the organisation.

Each of these aspects of the risk management process is discussed in more depth later in the chapter.

How to facilitate a successful risk management programme

If you are asked to facilitate risk or other workshops this should be regarded as a very positive measure of your reputation as someone trustworthy and competent to complete the role. Facilitation is a skill that can be learned and taking some time to learn these skills will pay dividends. The workshop may be part of your Control Risk Self Assessment (CRSA) process or could be established to assess a particular project or activity, for example, a systems development project or a risk assessment of the procurement activity.

Whatever the reason for the workshop, the basics will be the same. The following dos and don'ts are based on many years of experience and following these guidelines will provide a successful template.

THE DOS OF SUCCESSFUL RISK WORKSHOPS

- invite the optimum number of people;
- invite personnel who are peers or near peers;
- have very clear ground rules;
- hold the workshop without sending a detailed agenda in advance;
- have clear deliverables;
- issue the output very quickly;
- keep in control;
- finish at the advertised time.

The above suggestions can all be expanded on, as below.

- The optimum number of attendees at a risk workshop session is between ten and 16. Less than ten attendees could restrict the number of risks identified and the debate regarding their mitigation. More than 16 tends to become unwieldy.
- Inviting personnel who are peers or near peers ensures that everyone should contribute – no one will feel intimidated or awkward. Someone who is four levels or grades below other attendees is unlikely to feel comfortable in challenging the others.
- Have very clear ground rules and communicate these to the attendees at the start of the workshop. It may be sensible to have the most senior person explain these rules. Adopting the following ground rules will significantly enhance the benefits gained and the output from the workshop. It goes without saying that all of these statements must be believed.
  - Park your egos outside the door – it is probably better to explain this as 'seniority, and so on, is unimportant in the workshop'.
  - Everybody's contribution is welcomed equally.

- Nothing you say will be used in evidence against you – to ensure people have the confidence to highlight risks, concerns regarding controls, and so on, in an open and honest manner.
- There will be no retribution if it is found that controls are considered capable of improvement; it is not an intention to apportion blame. No 'witch hunting' will be allowed.
- There is no hidden agenda; this is not a disguised attempt at cost reduction – the workshop is purely to enable the organisation to evaluate the key risks and to assess how well they are being managed.
- If you can do so try to avoid sending out a detailed agenda – particularly if the attendees are senior and are used to having a meeting agenda. You want to create a different environment and demonstrate that a risk workshop is a chance to look at the business differently.
  - You want this experience to be very positive (counter cultural, if necessary).
  - You want to make the attendees think.
  - You want them to look at the business from a different perspective.
  - You want the people attending to bring their brains.

NB It is, of course, important that the facilitator has a very clear idea of the workshop outline and its timings.

The Risk-based Auditing Toolkit, Section 2 provides an example memo (see Appendix).

- It is very important to have clear deliverables. A memo sent out by a Director (ideally the CEO) explaining these deliverables and posing some questions to get the attendees thinking is an excellent idea.

The Risk-based Auditing Toolkit, Section 3 provides a suggested outline (see Appendix).

- Issue the output very quickly. You need to have someone standing by to write up the output and issue it within 24 hours whilst the ideas are still fresh in the minds of the attendees.
- Keep in control. You will need to know how to:
  - keep to time;
  - deal with conflicts;
  - stop attendees monopolising the discussions;
  - ensure all personnel have their say;
  - clarify any misunderstanding;
  - help ensure risks and not controls are identified initially;
  - mediate if necessary;
  - explain terminology;
  - keep the group focused, summarise and recap;
  - offer ideas;
  - act as devil's advocate.

THE DON'TS OF SUCCESSFUL RISK WORKSHOPS

- do not schedule more than half a day for the workshop;
- don't issue a list of risks first;
- don't have too long between workshops;
- don't allow one or two personnel to dominate;
- don't allow rambling and unfocused debate;
- don't expect everyone will be 100 per cent enthusiastic.

Again, the above list of don'ts can be expanded as seen below.

- Do not schedule a workshop for more than half a day. Firstly it is unlikely that personnel will want to attend for longer than a few hours and also the concentration and focus wavers considerably after half a day. The optimum solution for risk workshops is to have two half-day sessions a week or so apart (09.00–12.30 or 13.30–17.00 are usually good timings). The first should be used to identify and measure the risks and the second should assess the mitigation, identify exposures and latent opportunities and develop action plans.
- Do not issue a list of risks first. Whilst this is tempting, it is always counterproductive in my experience, as it is very difficult for personnel to think of any other risks when confronted with a list of, say, 40 or more risks.
- Do not have too long between the workshops. The workshops should be held close enough together to keep up the momentum but long enough to allow the attendees to research the processes actually in place to mitigate the risk before the second session. Equally, if you are intending to have a series of workshops with different levels of management, aim to complete the whole process within as short a period as practicable (not longer than two to three months altogether).
- Do not allow one or two personnel to dominate. Interestingly, it is not usually the most senior person who tries to dominate but may be the ambitious attendees who are keen to demonstrate their understanding and knowledge. You need to be able to deal quietly but strongly with such attempts to monopolise the arena.
- Equally you need to ensure that the debate is focused and delegates do not use the workshop to highlight some petty grievance or irrelevant issues.
- Do not expect everyone to be totally enthusiastic. You will know who they are! They will either question the need for the workshop loudly, complain there are better uses of their valuable time or simply sit there with their arms folded.

  If you can bring these people into the conversation, highlight the benefits from their perspective, focus on areas of opportunity, and so on, they may mellow. Often these 'Doubting Thomases' are the most enthusiastic as the workshop progresses as they begin to see the benefits for their own area. It is a very good idea to nurture these people as they will then become ambassadors for the process highlighting the benefits to other departments.

FACILITATING WORKSHOPS

The following outline provides a good template for facilitation training:

Risk facilitation

INTRODUCTION AND CONTEXT

- objectives;
- the characteristics of effective risk management;
- breaking down the barriers;
- Corporate Governance and prudential requirements;
- explanation of CRSA;
- specific aspects of risk management in the insurance sector;
- jargon busting – to develop a common language.

THE WORKSHOP PROCESS

- responsibilities of risk facilitator/co-ordinator;
- setting up workshops;
- determining attendees;
- setting objectives;
- tools and materials required;
- preparation of detailed agenda with timings;
- food for thought and diagnostic questions.

THE WORKSHOPS

- introductions and objectives;
- ground rules;
- skills required;
- the facilitator role;
- leading the workshop;
- explaining each activity;
- collating the input;
- clarifying misunderstandings;
- explanation of risk categories;
- aggregation of output;
- issuing of output to delegates;
- risk terminology explanation;
- helping attendees to identify risks, not effects of risks;
- explaining the need to identify inherent risks;
- risk assessment and categorisation;
- timekeeping;
- guillotining (stopping the discussions);
- ensuring all attendees have their say;
- encouraging full participation;
- keeping people on track;
- stopping attendees monopolising the discussions;
- mediating if necessary.

THE FIRST WORKSHOP – RISK IDENTIFICATION

- risk identification – individual brainstorm;
- collation and sifting;
- use of risk categories;
- risk clustering;
- feedback and group discussion;
- risk matrices;
- measurement and prioritisation;
- recording and reporting.

THE SECOND WORKSHOP – RISK MITIGATION

- collation of output from first workshop;
- how to ensure that participants research mitigation;
- discussion of risk mitigation;
- record agreed controls;
- identification of exposures;
- identification of opportunities;
- action plans;
- ownership;
- risk register preparation and issue.

ROLLING OUT A PROGRAMME

- developing the programme;
- how to keep up the impetus;
- the need for regular reporting;
- risk ownership and self certification;
- follow up.

LEADING THE WORKSHOP

The first and most important piece of advice is to remember that you are not acting as an Internal Auditor but as an independent referee/leader and the objective is to help the group to identify as many relevant risks as possible and evaluate the procedures to mitigate them.

The two key roles in leading a workshop are:

- to provide guidance and advice on the process for identifying risks, controls, exposures and opportunities;
- to manage the group involved to ensure the stated objectives are met.

The key is to ensure that the workshop is managed effectively but without fuss.

Explain each activity

Give an outline of the workshop and the key activities as they are reached, explaining the terminology and giving examples where necessary.

Collate the output

Draw together the issues, ensuring that there are no gaps, or if there are, who will be responsible for filling them.

Arrange the write up of the output, which should be organised in advance of the workshop rather than dropping the task on someone at the end.

Clarify misunderstandings

This can be a particularly important aspect of the role. There are invariably misunderstandings about:

- the need to hold workshops at all;
- the fact that risks are dealt with all the time, so they are self evident to the people involved;
- the breadth of risk; often attendees assume that health & safety and insurance are all that is to be covered;
- the difference between inherent and residual risks;
- the belief that risk is all negative: about problems, disasters and the undesirable;
- the need to identify strategic risks;
- the fact that certain risks are outside the control of the organisation but are no less important.

Explain risk categories

Many different ways of categorising risks can be used. I favour the following:

- strategic
- operational
- reputational
- financial
- regulatory
- IT and information
- people.

Whichever categories are used (I would strongly recommend not having more than ten or so), ensure that you are consistent with the explanations and use the same categories across the organisation.

Aggregate output

The facilitator will need to explain to the attendees how the output of the workshop will be aggregated with the other workshops' results and how strategic risks will be highlighted to the Board and operational risks pushed down to those who can directly influence them.

Risk terminology

The definitions and explanation of each aspect of the risk management process must be given. These will include:

- risk

- risk transfer
- inherent risk
- residual risk
- mitigation
- exposures
- impact
- likelihood.

Help attendees to identify the actual risks

Giving examples of risks can be useful for providing guidance such as prefixes which generally precede risks such as:

- loss of
- lack of
- damage to
- failure of
- ineffective
- inefficient.

The message to give is that if you can put the words above before the issue the likelihood is that they will have identified a specific risk.

It is also important to urge the group to identify risks as specifically as possible; broad generalisations such as damage to reputation will not prove to be a great deal of benefit. By way of explanation urge the attendees to identify 'damage to reputation caused by ...'

Inherent risks

This is often one of the most confusing aspects of a risk workshop. The way to describe an inherent risk is to consider how bad the impact could be if the procedures were ineffective. The inherent risk is therefore the gross risk or the worst-case scenario.

Time-keeping and guillotining

It is crucial that the session finishes on time. The facilitator may therefore have to guillotine sessions to ensure that the overall objective is met. This needs to be done sensitively. It is a very good idea to have a dummy workshop with Internal Audit staff beforehand to build a clear picture of timings.

Ensure all have their say

You need to go out of your way to bring everyone into the conversation. Watch carefully for those who are not saying much and encourage their comments.

Mediate

If a conflict occurs, it is the facilitator's job to take charge and resolve the situation. This is particularly difficult if the personnel involved are more senior than the facilitator, but you need to stay in charge.

Offer ideas

A good way of stimulating the attendees thought processes is to throw in ideas or challenges.

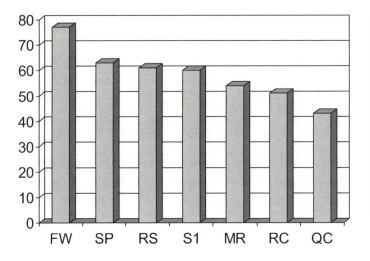

FW	=	Facilitated workshop
SP	=	Scenario planning
RS	=	Risk surveys and studies
SI	=	Structured interviews
MR	=	Management reports
RC	=	Risk committees
QC	=	Questionnaires and checklists

Source: Combination of surveys of risk assessment methods 2002–4

Figure 3.2   Effectiveness of risk identification methods

Risk identification

The key to successful risk identification is to start with a clean slate. The facilitator can throw in ideas which should be subject areas, for example, 'What are the regulatory risks?' rather than very specific (otherwise the facilitator could be accused of identifying the risks himself or herself).

Identifying the risks by means of a risk workshop is the method I would recommend, because, as the following chart shows, it is consistently highlighted by management as the most effective method. Seventy-seven per cent stated that this was successful whilst only 43 per cent regarded sending out questionnaires as a successful method.

Whichever method (or combination of methods) is chosen, a clear and consistent approach is needed to measure the risk.

NB Scenario planning is a very effective approach to evaluate specific risks identified after the workshop, especially for contract or project risks.

Measurement of risk

Risk can only be measured in two ways – firstly, the impact or consequences on the organisation if the event occurs and, secondly, the likelihood or probability of that event occurring. Impact can of course be financial, but it could also be related to reputation or damage the reputation. It may also be related to a major regulatory breach, or many other factors. Likelihood is generally related to time, how often is this event likely to occur, is it likely to be once a year, once every two years or once in 'a blue moon'.

An analogy will illustrate why most organisations think they understand risk but in practice probably don't. I use the analogy of driving a car. Most people, of course, do drive a car. If the question is asked 'What is the biggest risk in driving a car?' many people think initially that the main risk could be other drivers – a very convenient but erroneous assertion. The reality, of course, is that the ultimate risk in driving a car is being in an accident that causes your death. So in looking at the two measures of risk, the first question would be 'How likely is it that you would be in an accident that causes your death?' and the answer is hopefully, very unlikely. Is it an increasing likelihood however? Well certainly it would appear to be with more and more cars on the road. It cannot, however, be seen as likely otherwise no one would feel comfortable in driving a car.

The next question is 'Are there actions we could take to reduce the likelihood of being in an accident that causes our death?' Well there are. The first action, of course, would be to drive within the speed limits. How many of us can say that we have never exceeded the speed limit? Secondly, obey all the regulations, for example, not using a mobile phone when driving. Speed cameras and speed bumps are also put in place to reduce the likelihood, but there is one other action that is statistically guaranteed to reduce the likelihood of having a fatal accident, but it is one that very few drivers take. The answer is to take an advanced driving test. How many of you reading this have taken such a test? Very few of you, I'm sure, yet this is guaranteed to reduce the chances of your having an accident. In fact, insurance companies will give you reduced premiums, if you have passed this test. (NB This test is available in many European countries, but certainly not worldwide.)

Let's look at the other measure, the impact. What could reduce the impact if you were in an accident? Firstly, there are the safety features such as airbags, collapsible steering wheels, and so on, but probably the most important is wearing of seat belts. So another question for you – have you been in a taxi recently and not put your seatbelt on? I'm sure that a large proportion of readers are nodding. The taxi is certainly not safe enough to remove the need for a seatbelt. In fact, in many countries, it is illegal not to wear them.

Now, apart from illustrating the two measures of risk, what this analogy hopefully illustrates is that in our everyday lives we do not take these issues seriously enough and we know we should, then the chances are that your organisation is doing the same. If you need anything to sell the benefits of formalised risk management the above should provide you with some ammunition.

The risk management programme

Many organisations will by now have introduced a formal programme to evaluate and record their most significant risks. But has this been a positive experience?

- Can you demonstrate measurable benefits as a result?
- Did your organisation embrace the need enthusiastically or did they regard this as another passing fad – yet another initiative?
- Have you identified new areas of exposure?
- Have you identified any over controlled activities – and taken action to reduce the unnecessary controls?
- Or have you just ticked the boxes?

It is becoming increasingly apparent that the keys to success in this arena, as in many others, are people and process.

It is not too late. If the top management buy in has not been positive, develop a short awareness presentation for them – as specific as possible to your sector and experiences; hit them between the eyes, ask them how sure they are that such events could not occur or recur.

My experience of facilitating risk management programmes for organisations in both the private and public sectors provides some clear themes. In relation to identification of key risks the ones ever present in the critical impact category (boxes 9, 8, 7 and 6 of the matrix in Figure 3.3) are the following:

- failure to manage projects effectively;
- loss of IT systems;
- failure of partners or inability to establish effective partnering;
- loss of key personnel;
- damage to reputation due to loss of trust;
- hacking/breach of system security;
- failure to innovate;
- poor prioritisation of systems development;
- loss of morale/stress;
- too much data – insufficient information.

All these risks relate directly to either people or process (or, of course, both). The key to success is to recognise the link between these factors and to manage the relationship effectively.

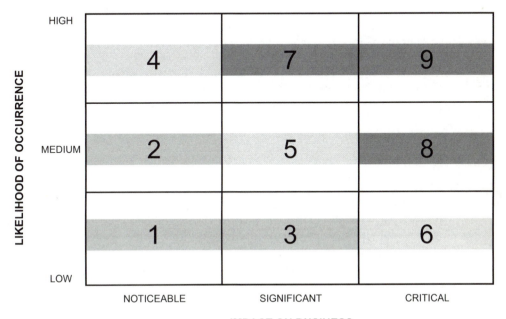

Figure 3.3   Risk matrix

People and process risks

FAILURE TO MANAGE PROJECTS EFFECTIVELY

This risk is one that is often poorly mitigated. By means of illustration, how many IT system development projects do you know that have been delivered on time, to budget and fully met the needs of the users?

LOSS OF KEY IT SYSTEMS

This risk is normally well managed by means of back up disciplines and business continuity plans using a mix of hot and cold start facilities. The aspects that are invariably less well considered are the people issues – if you lose an office housing other than IT facilities where do the personnel go to continue their work?

FAILURE OF PARTNERS

Much can be done to reduce the impact of failure of key partners, whether this is a failure in performance or the organisation ceasing to trade. The key is of course in the selection of the partner and in the performance contract established, but how many organisations have evaluated viable alternatives should the worst happen?

LOSS OF KEY PERSONNEL

Organisations generally identify the implications of the loss of top management as a risk, but how many recognise the critical impact of the loss of an 'expert' in IT, production control or another very technical discipline?

DAMAGE TO REPUTATION DUE TO LOSS OF TRUST

Ask Gerald Ratner about the penalties for saying too much to the media. And the implications for ex-employees of Andersens of shredding documents. All such events and many others too numerous to mention here all relate to one issue – people – what they do or don't do.

FAILURE TO INNOVATE

'The ultimate risk is not taking a risk,' said James Goldsmith. Many organisations fail to recognise that innovation is a lifeline, especially in times of consolidation. It needs vision, foresight and courage – which is why the most successful organisations in the world are usually those that embrace risk rather than try to avoid it.

The common theme from all the above risks, I believe, is trust. Whether the risk relates to information, systems, finance, marketing, regulation, strategy or any other source the common link is trust; the application or the breach thereof.

Risk management can therefore be regarded as the extent to which all aspects of trust are managed.

Engaging management

Identifying the risks is just the tip of the iceberg, evaluation of the processes to mitigate the threats and determining the exposures and opportunities is the key – and then implementing actions to address the exposures and exploit the opportunities.

The main responsibility for both risk ownership and implementation of the actions from the risk management programme rests with operational management – they are in this respect, as in many others, the first line of defence – the trusted generals and soldiers – and they are the difference between success and failure in embedding a risk management process. The risk management programme is a CRSA (Control Risk Self Assessment) process, whereby management take accountability and responsibility for the risks under their control and should thereafter be held to account for demonstrating that such risks are being appropriately managed (often being required to sign off on an annual basis to this effect).

If they have not fully bought into the process, no amount of leadership from the top will compensate. It is, therefore, important to involve operational management at the earliest possible opportunity, stressing to them that risk management is a method of helping them to achieve their objectives, reduce bureaucracy and remove unnecessary procedures rather than being additional work for them. Only they can embed the risk management process within the organisation by:

- linking the output into the planning and budgeting processes;
- sharing best practice with other functions;
- working together with other functions to address exposures identified in business interfaces;
- supporting senior management to implement the strategic actions identified during the risk evaluations.

Spend time reinforcing the following benefits of risk management to them:

- reduces the chance of surprises;
- enhances achievement of objectives;
- facilitates better planning;
- allows best practice to be shared;
- encourages people to think;
- promotes ownership – gives you more control of your own destiny;
- enhances consistency;
- promotes positive culture change;
- ensures more informed decisions;
- enhances communication;
- helps break down the 'silos';
- breeds more openness;
- ensures more winners are backed.

Whilst there are a myriad of issues to consider when looking at an effective risk management process, the real key to success is recognising that you need a solution that is specific to your organisation. If you manage the people and process aspects well and engage your operational management by demonstrating trust in them you are almost guaranteed success.

Risk mitigation

The only real piece of jargon that is needed in relation to risk management is the distinction between an inherent and a residual risk. An inherent risk is the pure risk, the gross risk, the risk before controls or mitigation. This might seem a rather difficult concept and can be awkward to address in risk workshops. The inherent risks will be identified in the first workshop and the residual risks in the second (when the mitigation for each risk is evaluated). The risk mitigation workshops tend to be quite different in format from the initial session when the risks are identified.

Functional specialists should be involved as it is critical to have these personnel in attendance with their specific in-depth knowledge of the risk areas. It would make no sense to have the HR manager trying to assess the mitigation for the IT risks.

It is sensible to mix the specialists with general management in small groups of three to five as this provides the opportunity for challenge. Otherwise the functional management may be tempted to overstate the effectiveness of the mitigation procedures.

The risks will then be rescored using the matrix in Figure 3.3 to arrive at the residual risks. The bigger the difference between the inherent and residual scores the more important the control (or mitigation procedures), as illustrated by Figure 3.4.

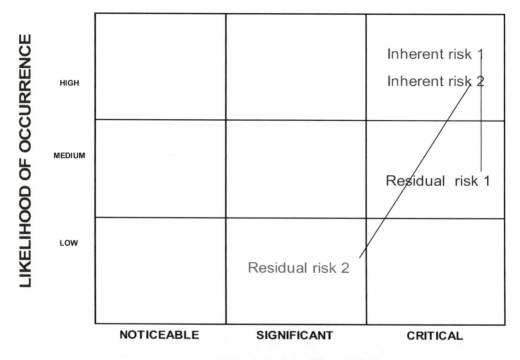

Figure 3.4   Risk assessment matrix: inherent and residual risk

Assessing actual versus perceived controls

When carrying out an audit of the area at a later date, you will be able to assess the controls actually in place and compare this with management's own evaluation. In the example above risk 2 could be an area where management are congratulating themselves on the risk having been very well managed. If, during the audit, you find significant gaps in the controls or poor compliance, the risk may well leap back up to the inherent level, that is, the top right hand box of the matrix.

The message you need to give management in these circumstances is that the residual risk is actually much higher than they believe and urgent action is necessary to deal with the situation.

In this way the true aspect of risk-based audit emerges:

- the independent audit assessment of both the risks and controls that were originally evaluated by management themselves;
- providing clear guidance on the actions to take to deal with the resultant exposures.

Risk exposures

The exposures identified by management in the workshops or alternatively by the Internal Auditors during their audits can be dealt with in one of four ways. This is often referred to as the 4 Ts.

Treating Risk Exposures

The 4 Ts

Tolerate ... accept the risk (self insurance)
          for example, by covering a large car fleet third party only

Transfer ... let someone manage the risk on your behalf
          for example, by insurance or outsourcing non-core activities such as IT

Terminate ... eliminate the risk
          for example, by withdrawing a problematic product

Treat ... take cost-effective in-house actions to reduce the risks
          for example, by carrying long lead time products in several warehouses

---

Risk registers

The usual output from a risk programme is a risk register (sometimes referred to as a risk map).

The Risk-based Auditing Toolkit, Section 4 provides a typical layout (see Appendix).

It is important to recognise that this is not a static profile, risks will vary in terms of their impact and likelihood and new risks will emerge on a regular basis. The role of the risk owners (one should be identified for each risk), is to take responsibility for the update of the register for risks under their control. They should also be required to notify other departments or functions regarding processes which are interdependent as the risk profiles change.

Monitoring management action plans

Another role often undertaken by Internal Audit is to assess the progress on the actions established during the workshops to deal with risk exposures or exploit opportunities.

A periodic follow-up (say quarterly) and onward reporting (to the Board or Risk Management Committee) can help to ensure that the actions are given the appropriate amount of attention and priority.

The need to enhance the skills base

In order for Internal Audit to carry out the risk-based role – widening the coverage, facilitating workshops and maybe even carrying out audits by means of a workshop – a much broader set of skills is required. Not only has this increased the demand for auditors with a broader set of skills, it has also widened the pool of potential applicants and with it the career potential for auditors.

The Institute of Internal Auditors, having also recognised this fact, commissioned a very significant research project, which culminated in the publishing of the 'Competency Framework for Internal Auditing'.

The authors, William Birkett, Mona Barbera, Barry Leithhead, Marian Lower and Peter Roebuck are all highly experienced professionals and the resultant framework offers an extensive and highly relevant template for developing Internal Auditors.

THE COMPETENCY FRAMEWORK (CFIA)

The framework examines the challenges faced by the modern Internal Auditor and provides a structured set of roles and competencies, based on three elements of the Internal Auditors lifecycle – the new joiner (described as the entering Internal Auditor), one with two or three years' experience (the competent Internal Auditor) and Internal Audit management.

The elements of the key business processes form the basis of the framework. These are translated into units. The Competency Framework fully recognises the importance of risk and assurance as the following extracts from Units 1 and 4 show:

Unit 1. Develop understanding within the organisation about the risks associated with its functioning and contexts.

1.1 Understand an organisation's objectives/strategies, process capabilities and contextual dynamics.

1.2 Profile the organisation's attitude/stance on risk.

1.3 Understand the risk management strategies of the organisation.

1.4 Provide advice/recommendations relating to the organisation's risk management philosophies and strategies and their implementation.

Unit 4. Provide ongoing assurance to the organisation that is 'in control' relative to its risks.

4.1 Establish assurance strategies/plans.

4.2 Establish the scope of assurance projects.

4.3 Identify/develop the methodologies relevant to an assurance project.

4.4 Establish a project plan.

4.5 Conduct the assurance work.

4.6 Communicate the results with relevant parties.

Any assurance function embracing the framework embodied within CFIA will not just achieve best practice, but will be in a position to build long-term credibility and trust. It will also significantly aid their aspirations to play a key role in the full assurance agenda.

For full details of the Competency Framework visit the Institute of Internal Auditors' main website (www.theiia.org).

A number of very important elements in the transition from systems-based to risk-based assurance were identified during the research:

- **From control focus to risk focus**

  If there was no risk there would be no need for control. It is not possible to evaluate control effectively without analysing risk.

- **From risk to contexts**

  Organisations are exposed to risk from the conditions and circumstances (and the changes to these situations) which surround the organisation. The source of risk exposures and opportunities are the focus for risk analysis. These conditions, circumstances, threats and opportunities represent the contexts which have the potential to impact the organisation. Internal Audit must increasingly examine these contexts.

- **From past to future**

  Only a focus on the future when reviewing records, and so on, will drive performance and enhance control. Internal Auditors must become anticipators of future contexts and risks.

- **Review to preview**

  Internal Audit gains no credit by critiquing the past whilst managers face the challenge of the future. Much more emphasis on 'preview' must be made.

- **Auditing knowledge to business knowledge**

  Auditors need more and more real current knowledge of the business if they are to provide an effective service – particularly if they intend to widen the coverage – as per the risk-based approach. Being a competent auditor and understanding how to carry out an audit is no longer enough.

- **Imposition to invitation**

  The more requests an Internal Audit function receives the better its reputation and the more it is trusted. Internal Audit increasingly needs to be demand rather than supply driven.

- **Persuasion to negotiation**

  It is important that the auditor is persuasive in both audit meetings and the report, but it is very important to recognise that the best solutions usually come through negotiation. It is important that the auditor offers options or alternative solutions to ensure that the best overall solution is sought.

How to undertake a skills inventory

Given the much more challenging environment for the modern Internal Auditor it is important to evaluate both the skills required and determine how the team measures up. The following is a very good exercise to complete each year.

Using the schedule of skills below, which are the top 20 identified by the Internal Audit functions in the Business Risk Management Ltd database, assess your team members against each and score each auditor out of 10.

Identify the gaps and areas for improvement and target training to deal with these opportunities. Add on other skills if you regard these as particularly important to your environment. It is of course not necessary that all auditors have all the skills (or in the same degree).

The top 20 skills (in no particular order) are:

- communication skills – written
- communication skills – oral
- communication skills – auditory
- communication skills – facilitation
- communication skills – presentation
- broad business knowledge
- IT awareness
- results orientation
- negotiation
- open-mindedness
- self control
- diplomacy
- analytical skills
- healthy scepticism
- experience in risk and controls
- eagle-eyed
- flexibility and adaptability
- planning
- self motivation
- decision-making ability.

An example skills evaluation with a number of the actions highlighted is shown in the Risk-based Auditing Toolkit, Section 5 (see Appendix).

INTERPERSONAL AWARENESS – HOW TO PREPARE

Given that interpersonal awareness is a critical aspect of the modern audit role the more preparation the better. A key element of the audit process is to deal effectively with the key site personnel. This can be achieved by learning as much as you can about the key contacts – by speaking to audit managers and the personnel responsible for that location. It is also important to recognise that cultural or regional differences can impact on the success of the audit assignment. Therefore if you are visiting another country you need to prepare even more thoroughly (especially if it is your first time visiting that location).

- Speak to nationals of the country within your team where possible to learn about the 'dos and don'ts'.
- Visit the website of your embassy in the country to be visited or other useful sites (lists should be kept in the public folders).
- Go out of your way to make the first contact positive (arranging pre-meeting, and so on). Stress that you will be trying to minimise disruption, respect local customs and ask for their advice in this regard.
- Demonstrate language skills if you have them.
- Follow the guidelines for success consistently:
  - Respect and understand cultural differences.
  - Be open and flexible to other ways and approaches.
  - Don't be over-eager to compare methods to those in your own country.
  - Recognise and applaud positive practices.
  - Don't pretend that you know it all.
  - Keep your ego under wraps.
  - Be warm and friendly.
- Check the public holidays. Also, in some countries, notably in the Middle East, be sure you take account of the different working week; in this part of the world Thursday and Friday are the weekend.
- Ensure that you recognise potential language difficulties.

Even with this resource available you will have difficulty in obtaining full descriptions and understanding of the processes in place. The suggested technique is to ask more than one person the same set of questions. This will not only help to ensure understanding is consistent, but will allow further questioning if responses are different, thereby ensuring the accuracy of both the information given and its translation.

4 *Risk-based Audit Planning*

Risk-based strategic audit planning

Determining the areas to audit is the first stage of the Risk-based Audit methodology.

This can be seen diagrammatically in The Risk-based Auditing Toolkit, Section 6 (see Appendix).

The risk-based audit approach is to focus the audit effort primarily towards the most significant risks faced by the business. It is recognised, however, that the capability of Internal Audit to audit some activities, notably those of a technical or highly complex nature, is a key factor.

There is therefore a need to be able to determine the priorities for audit attention in a structured and consistent manner. The rationale for choosing the specific audits needs to be supportable and evidenced, rather than being based purely on 'gut-feel'. A number of steps are necessary to develop a robust process:

- Prepare a schedule of all possible audit topics – usually known as the Audit Universe.
- Get as much input as possible from management as to the topics which they regard as important. The risk register (if one has been completed) will provide a good source of information.
- Determine the level of assurance management want from you.
- Decide the minimum frequency of audits acceptable to senior management and the Audit Committee.
- Assess the skills available to you and the depth of business knowledge to deliver assignments, notably those where technical knowledge is required.
- Combine all this information into a robust evaluation to determine audit priorities.

Determining the audit universe

The audit universe is the complete schedule of all possible audit topics. This schedule should include both audit types and the locations at which such assignments could be completed.

The more effort taken to create the audit universe the better. It should be a full list of all possible audits even if there is no intention currently (or insufficient resources) to audit them all. The reason is that the Board and the Audit Committee should be just as interested in the audits you are not planning to tackle as this will impact on the overall level of assurance you are able to provide.

The following template (or a similar format) should be developed:

Audit Activities	Location 1	Location 2	Location 3	Location 4	Location 5	Location 6	Head Office	Regional Office 1
1	X		X			X		
2				X	X	X		
3		X	X	X	X	X		
4							X	
5							X	X
6	X						X	
7		X	X					
8		X	X	X				
9	X	X	X	X	X			
10	X	X	X	X	X	X		
11							X	X
12							X	
13	X		X		X			
14		X	X		X	X		
15	X	X		X				
16			X	X				
17	X							
18				X	X	X		
19	X	X	X	X	X	X		
20		X	X	X	X	X		

Figure 4.1   Audit universe model

Translating key risks from the business risk process into the basis of the audit programme

Getting management's list of audit priorities is a crucial step in developing an effective audit plan. As most of the risks should have been identified by management, the risk register and the risk matrix will be invaluable in this regard.

The most significant inherent risks (not the residual risks) should form the primary focus for Internal Audit attention. The inherent risks should be used because the audit will

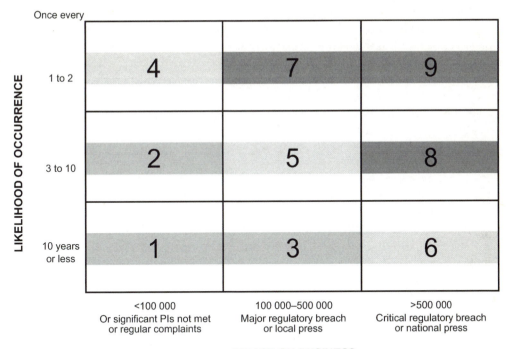

Figure 4.2   Risk assessment matrix

evaluate the effectiveness of the controls in place and therefore confirm or otherwise the remaining or residual risk.

The most significant risks as per the matrix above are those in boxes 6 to 9. Box 6 is included in addition to the red risks (boxes 7 to 9) as the risks in this category are of critical impact but are unlikely to occur – 'the disaster scenario'.

Whilst the highest inherent risks are likely to represent the key audit topics it is also important to give the less risky areas some attention.

The reason is that the risks in the green zone (boxes 1 to 3) are often the audits which will identify the greatest opportunities, as these can often be areas that are over-managed or over-controlled. As an example, imagine an area of the business which poses a small level of inherent risk (low impact and medium likelihood – a score of 2 on the risk matrix) but there are eight separate controls in place in mitigation. It may be that the level of control is excessive.

Imagine the positive reaction from management if you identified unnecessary controls or over-managed activities and were able to make recommendations for their removal or simplification.

Determining the level of assurance required

The level of assurance required by management will influence the depth of the audit and the amount of testing required. It is therefore very important that areas are identified where higher levels of assurance than normal are expected. Audit management will determine such issues in discussion with senior management.

Perhaps unexpectedly to some readers, the majority of audits will only provide a relatively low level of assurance. Furthermore management will be quite comfortable with this situation. Some of the reasons for this are as follows:

- Management need to be relied upon to manage their activities. If the activity is well established and well managed with a stable team in place, senior management should be comfortable to rely mainly on the function itself to provide the majority of the assurance.
- Audit will only generally assess a small proportion of the total transactions processed.
- The audit will usually focus on a limited time period.

The level of assurance which can be provided by Internal Audit is therefore only additional rather than fundamental. The level of assurance can be enhanced by the use of computer-assisted audit techniques. The levels of control and the required testing to provide varying levels of assurance are detailed on the following pages.

Management should be asked if there are any specific audits where they require a relatively higher level of assurance, for example, for new activities such as e-commerce or areas where concerns have been expressed. Additional time will need to be factored into the plan for such assignments.

ASSESSING THE LEVEL OF ASSURANCE

One approach to assessing the level of assurance is to consider the different controls and how much testing will be carried out for each type. The following are the levels of control which should be taken into consideration.

Operating controls

These are the day-to-day controls, performed in real time by the originator of the transaction and for every transaction – an example might be a clerk checking a purchase invoice to the order and goods received note before passing the invoice for payment. Very rarely will Internal Audit be there whilst the original transaction is performed. The only possible exception may be attendance at a stocktaking or similar event.

Monitoring or supervisory controls

These are the controls applied by supervisors and are usually performed soon after the original transaction. An example would be a supervisor checking a batch of invoices prepared by a purchase ledger clerk. Again, it is unlikely that the auditor will be on-site whilst the supervisors are completing this task. It is, however, possible that the auditor might test check these controls.

Oversight controls

These are the management controls performed some time after the original transaction (for example at period end) on information passed to them by supervisors. An example would be checking to ensure that a bank reconciliation has been completed properly and to evidence this management control by means of signature or initials. Auditors would definitely review these controls but would be looking for evidence of the procedures being completed rather than re-performing the checks, that is, the auditor would not usually re-perform the bank reconciliation.

Governance controls

This is usually where modern Internal Audit focuses the majority of their efforts. Governance controls are the independent assessments completed by assurance providers (that is, those functions without direct operational responsibilities). Individual transactions are reviewed primarily to prove that the procedures are valid and being consistently applied. The focus is primarily on the design of controls rather than detailed transaction testing.

Table 4.1   Control evaluation and levels of assurance provided

Level of assurance	Operating controls	Monitoring controls	Oversight controls	Governance controls
Very low	No testing	No testing	No testing	High level testing
Low	No testing	No testing	High level testing	High level testing
Medium	No testing	High level testing	Detailed testing	In-depth testing
High	High level testing	Detailed testing	Detailed testing	In-depth testing
Very high	Detailed testing	Detailed testing	Detailed testing	In great depth

The depth of testing should be assessed against the chart. For example, if the audit is designed to review the high level governance and oversight controls, but no more detailed testing, a low level of assurance will be provided.

This should be no real surprise, for clearly the audit is carried out at a specific point in time and only a very small number of the transactions will be subject to review. As previously stated, the audit is only designed to provide an additional level of assurance in most cases as functional management (who are involved 365 days a year) provide the main assurance.

The main aspect of this evaluation is not to demean the importance of an Internal Audit but to ensure senior management recognise that the typical audit cannot provide unequivocal assurance (or anything similar).

The key planning aspect is to try and determine on an annual or semi-annual basis if there are any audit topics for which management require a higher level of assurance. Typically, these will represent areas of emerging or rapidly changing risk. For such topics a much more detailed audit will be required. As can be seen from the matrix, to take the level of assurance from low to high requires an in-depth analysis of governance controls and detailed testing of oversight and monitoring controls, which will involve much more time and effort.

There is an excellent and efficient way of enhancing the level of assurance. This is by the use of a Computer Assisted Audit Technique (CAAT), a software package such as ACL or IDEA. These excellent and well used tools are designed specifically for Internal Auditors and can be used to examine the whole population of transactions, rather than a sample, in order to pick out the exceptions, map the trends, and so on. Examining a complete population naturally allows a high level of assurance to be given.

This is, in my opinion, one of the most compelling and underappreciated reasons for investing in these products. To find more details about the software, visit the respective websites – www.acl.com and www.caseware-idea.com.

Determining minimum acceptable audit coverage

It is very common that certain audits will be required by senior management to be completed annually or even more frequently. Other less critical assignments will be covered perhaps every two or three years. It is generally recognised that covering topics less than once every three years is not credible from an overall assurance perspective. It is important to get the Board and the Audit Committee's agreement to the minimum coverage level, as this will determine the duration of the strategic plan. Three years is the most common period.

Determining audit priorities and developing the plan

The following risk model takes all the above factors into account and allows each potential audit to be compared with any other – to determine the audit priorities. It, therefore, takes into account a variety of factors in addition to the risk:

- relative value of expenditure or income;
- number of transactions processed;
- the quality and turnover of management and staff;
- the relative significance of external factors (partnerships, regulatory requirements, and so on);
- an evaluation of the standard of internal control;
- the likely effectiveness of an audit;
- the relative duration of the audit assignment;
- the length of time since the last audit;
- the level of assurance or otherwise provided by other independent evaluation providers, for example, external audit.

The duration of each assignment is determined by both past experience and the level of assurance required and the total resource requirements. It is then evaluated using the agreed cycle (for example, three years). The available resource can then be compared with that required to audit all topics and the difference (the lower priority audits) can be highlighted for senior management to discuss. The overall plan will then be arranged into annual chunks with a mix of topics each year, that is, all top priority audits will not be scheduled for Year 1.

The audit planning model was developed and is owned by Business Risk Management Ltd. It was originally developed in 1999 taking into account the best practice from other models and verifying the results with hundreds of Internal Audit functions. The model has been regularly updated and is used by at least 1200 Internal Audit functions across the world.

If you would like a free electronic copy of the model please contact me at pg@businessrisk.co.uk.

Audit risk analysis model

The model is predicated on the basis that all risks are relative but that they can be compared by combining three key factors:

1   The size of the risk or exposure.
2   The controls in place
3   The likely effectiveness of the audit.

Each of these three factors is given an equal overall weighting to reflect the fact that audit assessment is a combination of risk and control. Each factor is split into four sections as shown in Table 4.2.

Table 4.2   Factors in the audit risk analysis model

	Size	Controls	Effectiveness
A	Value of annual income, expenditure or size of budget		
B	Number of employees involved in the activity		
C	Impact score from the risk matrix		
D	Number of transactions		
F		Evaluation of the quality of management and staff	
G		Third Party sensitivity	
H		Standard of internal control	
J		Likelihood of occurrence as per risk matrix	
K			Likely effectiveness of Internal Audit
L			Duration of audit work
M			Time since last audit
N			Effectiveness of other assurance providers

Each topic in the audit universe is then evaluated to create a score for each of the sections above. The overall scores are combined to create an overall result which can then be ranked alongside the results for all the other potential audits.

   NB Functions or systems can be divided in any manner providing the whole business population is covered and the approach is consistent.

   The objective is to compare an audit topic against all other possible audits. It is suggested that this is carried out once a year by the Head of Internal Audit with his or her managers.

THE MODEL

1. SIZE: Parameters relating to the *size* of the exposure or risk

A = Value of annual income or expenditure, or size of budget

1: the smallest area of financial expenditure or income you could audit
2: the next largest area
3: the next largest
4: the next largest
5: the very largest area of financial expenditure or income you could audit

The financial categories and currency will need to be set specifically to suit the organisation. Example categories might be:

1: up to £2 m
2: between £2 m and £20 m
3: between £20 m and £100 m
4: between £100 m and £200 m
5: over £200 m

B = Number of employees involved in the activity

1: the smallest number of employees in any area that you could audit
2: the next largest
3: the next largest
4: the next largest
5: the very largest number of employees in any area that you could audit

The rationale is that the more employees are involved in processing transactions in the area under review, the greater the chance of error – and the greater the risk
    Example numbers of employees might be:

1: up to 10
2: between 11 and 50
3: between 51 and 100
4: between 101 and 200
5: over 201

NB the number of employees should be the number working in the function under review not the number of employees processed. For example, for the audit of payroll if there are 12 payroll personnel dealing with 20 000 employees the score in the above section would be two, that is, between 11 and 50 employees.

C = Impact score from the risk matrix

If your organisation has formally identified and prioritised its risks, the risk register can be used for this purpose. If not you will have to evaluate this yourself – or get management to give you their views during the strategic audit planning process.

C = Impact upon the organisation as per the risk matrix, that is, if something were to go wrong in the area under review what would be the biggest potential impact on the business.

1: negligible
2: small
3: significant
4: potentially serious
5: potentially disastrous

D = Number of transactions

1: smallest number of transactions processed in any business area
2: next smallest
3: average number of transactions
4: large number of transactions
5: largest number of transactions processed in any business area

The rationale is that the greater the number of transactions processed in the area under review, the greater the chance of error – and the greater the risk

D = Example number of transactions might be:

1: fewer than 499 per month
2: 500 to 2499 per month
3: 2500 to 4999 per month
4: 5000 to 14 999 per month
5: 15 000 or over per month

2. CONTROL: Parameters relating to the effectiveness of controls and *likelihood* of the risk materialising

F = Evaluation of the quality of management and staff

Each of the criteria in the box below should be considered relative to the area to be audited.

Extent of staff turnover
Length of time operation has been within the business
Degree of expressed concern by management
Extent of use of contract labour on sensitive systems
Management's attitude to risk taking
Morale of staff

F = Management and staff

Score on a range of '1' to '5' where '1' represents top quality management and staff, with low turnover of both, in an operation which has been in existence for more than three years and about which no known concern is being expressed. A score of 5 would be the total opposite – poor quality management and staff with high turnover in both, and so on. A score of 2 would be given if one of the criteria gave cause for concern and so on.

G = Third Party sensitivity

Third party sensitivity is the extent to which the activity under audit is managed in part by another organisation, as in partnerships, or is subject to external regulations, and so on.

Tax implications
Extent of regulatory requirements
Legal implications
Joint ventures and partnerships

G = Third Party sensitivity

Score on a range '1' to '5' where 1 means there are no tax, legal, regulatory or other third party implications and '5' means that very significant third party sensitivity is present.

H = Standard of internal control

The criteria in the box below will be evaluated, based on knowledge, and a score given relative to the resultant assessment of the overall standard of internal control.

Means of authority to commit (for example, none, sole, sole with review, dual, committee)	Extent of losses Scope for intentional manipulation Vulnerability to fraud
Degree of technical sophistication of systems	Extent to which standard systems are being used
Extent to which operating manuals are complied with	Extent of recent reorganisations and systems changes
Known factors which should ring warning bells	Reliability of last internal control review Extent of weaknesses highlighted in last internal control review
Strength of accounting systems	
Extent of formal procedures	

H = Standard of internal control

1: Excellent with no known re-organisations or systems changes; little known scope for intentional manipulation
2: Above average with standard systems in use throughout

3: Sound

4: Known or suspected to be weak

5: Known or suspected to be very unsound

In this section, as in all the others, if there is no information about internal control, for example, if the audit has never been attempted before, a mid score of 3 will be given. It should not be assumed that internal control is weak or indeed very good. After completing the audit the model can be updated.

J = Likelihood of occurrence as per risk matrix

If your organisation has formally identified and prioritised its risks, the risk register can again be used for this purpose. If not you will have to evaluate this yourself – or get management to give you their views during the strategic audit planning process.

J = Measure of likelihood of occurrence as per risk matrix

How likely is it that the risk evaluated in Category C will occur?

1: Rare

2: Unlikely

3: Possible

4: Likely

5: Almost certain

3. EFFECTIVENESS: Parameters relating to the *probability of unwanted consequences being detected* if they do materialise.

K = Likely effectiveness of Internal Audit

Evaluate the criteria in the box below and score accordingly.

Willingness and ability of customer to react positively to results of audit
Extent to which relevant specialist skills are available to Internal Audit
Ability to conduct a competent audit
The degree of need for thorough audit follow-up
The quality of Internal Audit systems documentation
Knowledge of business and experience of staff
Involvement and availability of management

K = Likely effectiveness of Internal Audit

Score on a range '1' to '5' with a score of '5' if there are no significant constraints that are likely to preclude doing an effective audit, that is, a well-established function with fully experienced and trained staff with a good knowledge of the business together with receptive and focused line management. A high score of 5 indicates that this is an audit that you want to do.

L = Duration of audit work

1: the largest amount of time you would ever spend on an audit
2: the next largest amount of time
3: the next largest
4: the next largest
5: the very smallest amount of time you would ever spend on an audit

Examples might be:

1 = over eight man weeks
2 = six–eight man weeks
3 = four–five man weeks
4 = two–three man weeks
5 = less than two man weeks

M = Time since last audit

1 = less than six months
2 = between six and 12 months
3 = between 12 and 18 months
4 = between 18 and 24 months
5 = more than 24 months or never audited

N = Effectiveness of other assurance providers

1 = regular compliance, QA and other audits with no significant findings
2 = regular compliance, QA and other audits with a few significant findings
3 = no other audit work completed
4 = regular compliance, QA and other audits with many significant findings
5 = continual significant problems identified by assurance reviews

FORMULA USED FOR CALCULATION OF OVERALL SCORE

The scores are entered into the model below (Figure 4.3). Certain of the criteria are weighted, for example, A is given a weighting of two whilst H has a weighting of three. This weighting reflects the relative importance of the criteria. The model has been completed as an example with a maximum score of five in each of the size sections and a mid score of three in the rest.

Each element (size, control and effectiveness) has a maximum score of 1, as can be seen in the model example for the size element. The basis of the scoring takes into account that each of the elements (size, control and detection) is given equal importance. The three scores are therefore multiplied together. In the example 1.00 x 0.60 x 0.60 = 0.36 or 36 per cent.

The result is then multiplied by a constant of 200. This figure has been chosen as it has been found by regular use of the model that the maximum score for almost any audit is 0.50. Multiplying by 200 therefore gives a schedule with a resultant maximum score of 100 (0.50 x 200).

	Score	Weight	Total	Maximum score	Actual score	Constant	Total score
Size	1 to 5	1, 2 or 3					
A Combined value of income and expenditure	5	2	10				
B Number of employees	5	1	5				
C Impact on the organisation from risk matrix	5	3	15				
D Volume of transactions	5	1	5				
Total size score	A+B	+C+D	35	35	1.00		
Control							
F Impact of management and staff	3	2	6				
G Third party sensitivity	3	1	3				
H Standard of internal control	3	3	9				
J Likelihood of occurrence from risk matrix	3	3	9				
Total control score	F+G	+H+J	27	45	0.60		
Effectiveness							
K Likely effectiveness of audit	3	1	3				
L Duration of the audit	3	2	6				
M Length of time since the last review	3	2	6				
N Effectiveness of other assurance providers	3	2	6				
Total effectiveness score	+K+L	+M+N	21	35	0.60		
Total overall score	Size score	X Control score	X Effectiveness score	0.36	200		72.00

Figure 4.3   Audit risk assessment model

RELATIVE AUDIT PRIORITY

If the audit scores:

>80	Top priority audit
60–79	Critical topic for review
40–59	Important to tackle
20–39	Lower priority but still valid audit topic
<19	Audit probably unnecessary

The overall results (for each audit evaluated) are then entered into an audit priority schedule (Table 4.3):

Table 4.3   Audit priority schedule

Audit topic	Score from model	Frequency per 3 year cycle	Number of locations	Man days per audit	Total man days
1	96	1	1	10	10
2	92	3	1	8	24
3	90	1	3	12	36
4					
5					
6					
7					
8					
9					
10					
11					
12					
13					
14					
15					
16					
17					
18					
19					
20					

Worked example of an audit assessment using the model

Irrespective of the organisation the audit of the treasury function is likely to be regarded as very important, and is one where external audit often require Internal Audit to carry out regular (often annual) reviews.

Following through the model using treasury as an example the results are as follows:

Size

Section A, the value of income and/or expenditure is likely to be one of the very largest you could audit.

Score 5

Section B, the number of employees – relatively few personnel are involved in the actual treasury operation.

Score 2

Section C, impact on the organisation from the risk matrix – clearly the potential impact (financially and otherwise) if something were to go wrong in treasury could be catastrophic.

Score 5

Section D, volume of transactions – a reasonably large volume of transactions are processed but much less than some other activities.

Score 3

The overall score in the size section is 0.86 (86 per cent) as is to be expected in such a critical function. If you based your evaluation solely on size and impact you would audit treasury and similar topics to the exclusion of almost everything else.

	Score	Weight	Total	Maximum score	Actual score	Constant	Total score
Size	1 to 5	1, 2 or 3					
A Combined value of income and expenditure	5	2	10				
B Number of employees	2	1	. 2				
C Impact on the organisation from risk matrix	5	3	15				
D Volume of transactions	3	1	3				
Total size score	A+B	+C+D	30	35	0.86		

Figure 4.4 Audit risk assessment model: worked example (1) – size factors

Control

Section F, evaluation of effectiveness of management and staff. In this case, it is known that the treasury function has recently had new management and almost all new staff. It is therefore felt to be a higher risk.

Score 4

Section G, third party sensitivity. The considerable external influence with counterparties, banks, and so on, leads to a high third party sensitivity.

Score 4

Section H, last audit. The last audit 22 months ago highlighted a number of key internal control failures and it is understood that not all have been addressed.

Score 4

Section J, likelihood of occurrence. The question to be asked is how likely is the impact identified in Category C to occur. How likely is it that a catastrophic impact could be caused? It is regarded as being unlikely.

Score 2

The overall score in the control section is 67 per cent, high but nowhere near as high as the impact score (largely due to the low likelihood that the risk highlighted in the size section will occur).

Effectiveness of the audit

Section K, likely effectiveness of audit. If we assume that your organisation is a bank, there should be nothing to stop the Internal Auditors carrying out a good audit.

		Score	Weight	Total	Maximum score	Actual score	Constant	Total score
	Control							
F	Impact of management and staff	4	2	8				
G	Third party sensitivity	4	1	4				
H	Standard of internal control	4	3	12				
J	Likelihood of occurrence from risk matrix	2	3	6				
	Total control score	F+G	+H+J	30	45	0.67		

Figure 4.5 Audit risk assessment model: worked example (1) – control factors

Score 5

(If you are not a bank or similar organisation the audit might be regarded as more complex or difficult and therefore be given a lower score.)

Section L, duration of the audit. A medium duration audit (four–five man weeks)

Score 3

Section M, length of time since last review. It is 22 months since the last audit.

Score 4

Category N, no other assurance providers have reviewed this area.

Score 3

The overall score in the detection section is 71 per cent, again a high score.

		Score	Weight	Total	Maximum score	Actual score	Constant	Total score
	Effectiveness							
K	Likely effectiveness of audit	5	1	5				
L	Duration of the audit	3	2	6				
M	Length of time since the last review	4	2	8				
N	Effectiveness of other assurance providers	3	2	6				
	Total effectiveness score	+K+L	+M+N	25	35	0.71		

Figure 4.6   Audit risk assessment model: worked example (1) – effectiveness factors

The three section scores are then multiplied together (as they are regarded as having equal weight) to give a total score of 0.408. The result is multiplied by 200. The final score in this case is a very high 81.63. If you refer to the final assessment of results section of the model, it can be seen that this audit scoring over 80 is a top priority audit.

	Score	Weight	Total	Maximum score	Actual score	Constant	Total score
Total overall score		Size score X	Control score X	Effectiveness score	0.408	200	81.63

Figure 4.7   Audit risk assessment model: worked example (1) – overall score

To illustrate how the same treasury audit need not necessarily come out as a top priority and could, indeed, be one of the lower priority audits in the schedule look at the following evaluation. All the scores but three are the same as the earlier evaluation of treasury, the size sector score is 86 per cent as it was before. In this example, however:

The management and staff are very well established and are regarded as top quality, no concerns are being expressed.   Section F   *Score 1.*

The standard of internal controls is regarded as excellent.   Section H   *Score 1.*

The last audit was carried out 11 months ago.   Section L   *Score 2.*

The overall score as a result of these three changes is reduced from 81.63 to just 34.00. This is clearly an area that does not need to be audited again for some time (unless the situation changes radically).

As can be seen the model factoring in both control and detection criteria creates a very potent and accurate evaluation (and a method of challenging the need for the annual reviews asked for by external audit if controls are excellent).

	Score	Weight	Total	Maximum score	Actual score	Constant	Total score
Size	1 to 5	1, 2 or 3					
A Combined value of income and expenditure	5	2	10				
B Number of employees	2	1	2				
C Impact on the organisation from risk matrix	5	3	15				
D Volume of transactions	3	1	3				
Total size score	A+B	+C+D	30	35	0.86		
Control							
F Impact of management and staff	1	2	2				
G Third party sensitivity	4	1	4				
H Standard of internal control	1	3	3				
J Likelihood of occurrence from risk matrix	2	3	6				
Total control score	F+G	+H+J	15	45	0.33		
Effectiveness							
K Likely effectiveness of audit	5	1	5				
L Duration of the audit	3	2	6				
M Length of time since the last review	2	2	4				
N Effectiveness of other assurance providers	3	2	6				
Total effectiveness score	+K+L	+M+N	21	35	0.60		
Total overall score	Size score X	Control score X	Effectiveness score	0.17		200	34.00

Figure 4.8   Audit risk assessment model: worked example (2)

The audit priority schedule

Having completed the schedule (which should have all the audits entered in order with the highest score from the model first, you are then in a position to decide how much of the universe you can cover.

Using the example schedule shown in Table 4.4:

The arrows indicate that there are other audit scores which are not shown here.

- The highest score from the 105 possible audits is 96 and the lowest is 19.
- Assume that the total available resource over the three years (excluding administration, training, holidays, and so on) is 800 auditor days.
- You need to have some of this time as contingency for work which cannot be planned such as investigations, and so on (typically 10 per cent is a good guide).
- In the example, this therefore leaves 720 available days.
- As can be seen from the schedule 720 days allows 66 of the 105 audits to be tackled.
- A major benefit of this approach is that it allows a discussion with senior management (or the Audit Committee) to be held.
- Your message to them will be that with the resources you have (or that are already planned) you will be able to complete 66 audits (or approximately 70 per cent of the audit universe).

If they are happy with this coverage all is well. You need, of course, to remind them that your annual assurance statement to them will be restricted to the audit areas covered. The Head of Internal Audit should always be encouraged to provide such an annual statement.

If senior management are not happy with the coverage (and in Table 4.4 with one third of the total universe not receiving any attention, they probably will not be happy) they have four options.

Table 4.4 Audit priority schedule: worked example

Audit topic	Score from model	Frequency per three-year cycle	Number of locations	Man days per audit	Total man days
1	96	1	1	10	10
2	92	3	1	8	24
3	90	1	3	12	36
	⇩	⇩	⇩	⇩	⇩
65	45	1	1	8	8
66	42	2	1	4	8
	⇩	⇩	⇩	⇩	⇩
					720

Contingency estimated 80

Total Available Resources 800

67	40	1	2	12	24
68	39	1	1	16	16
	⇩	⇩	⇩	⇩	⇩
103	20	1	3	4	12
104	19	1	1	7	7
105	19	1	1	8	8

Total Required Resources 1250

1   Give you more resources.
2   Reduce the number of locations to be visited. For example, in audit topic 3 on the schedule, if only two of the three locations were visited this would save 12 man days which could then be put towards audit topic 67.
3   Reduce the frequency of coverage. For example, audit topic 2 is scheduled to be audited once a year (that is, three times within the three-year cycle). If this was reduced to once every 18 months, eight man days would be released.
4   They could advise you which topic they would like to drop and which of the other audits they would want you to replace it with and why.

The beauty of the whole audit risk model approach is that:

- it is practical and consistent;
- it takes away much of the subjectivity or 'gut-feel';
- it is easily explained to management;
- it ensures that audit does not have to make all the decisions regarding priorities;
- it allows audit to make a good case for additional resources;
- it takes into account the key risks but also factors in the strength of controls and your ability to carry out an effective audit;
- it facilitates evaluation of audit requests as the position on the priority schedule can be used to allocate relative priority.

Which risks are not easily auditable?

Inevitably there will be a number of audits in the universe which are very much more complex than others to review effectively, or require much more technical know-how.

The audit risk model, if used correctly, should take care of these issues, in terms of relative priority on the resultant audit priority schedule. This can be illustrated with an example of an audit of network security, certainly one of the more technically-based assignments (Figure 4.9). In the first example it is assumed that you have an IT audit capability and have personnel with significant knowledge and skills of the technical aspects of IT.

As a result the audit can be completed fairly quickly.

Section K, likely effectiveness of audit   *Score 5.*
Section L, duration of the audit   *Score 4.*
Overall Score 51.00 – an important audit.

In the second example (Figure 4.10) (the same organisation) it is assumed that you have few if any specialist IT skills available and completing the audit would be a long and tortuous process.

Section K, likely effectiveness of audit   *Score 1.*
Section L, duration of the audit (twice as long as the first example)   *Score 2.*
Overall Score 37.00 – lower audit priority.

This of course in no way diminishes the importance of the audit itself but it is necessary to be practical, if you have limited resources it is better that you put them where they can do the most good.

	Score	Weight	Total	Maximum score	Actual score	Constant	Total score
Size	1 to 5	1, 2 or 3					
A Combined value of income and expenditure	3	2	6				
B Number of employees	2	1	2				
C Impact on the organisation from risk matrix	4	3	12				
D Volume of transactions	2	1	2				
Total size score	A+B	+C+D	22	35	0.63		
Control							
F Impact of management and staff	3	2	6				
G Third party sensitivity	4	1	4				
H Standard of internal control	2	3	6				
J Likelihood of occurrence from risk matrix	2	3	6				
Total control score	F+G	+H+J	22	45	0.49		
Effectiveness							
K Likely effectiveness of audit	5	1	5				
L Duration of the audit	4	2	8				
M Length of time since the last review	5	2	10				
N Effectiveness of other assurance providers	3	2	6				
Total effectiveness score	+K+L	+M+N	29	35	0.83		
Total overall score	Size score	X Control score	X Effectiveness score	0.255	200		51.00

Figure 4.9   Audit risk assessment model: network security (1)

	Score	Weight	Total	Maximum score	Actual score	Constant	Total score
Total size score	A+B	+C+D	22	35	0.63		
Total control score	F+G	+H+J	22	45	0.49		

Effectiveness

	Score	Weight	Total	Maximum score	Actual score	Constant	Total score
K Likely effectiveness of audit	1	1	1				
L Duration of the audit	2	2	4				
M Length of time since the last review	5	2	10				
N Effectiveness of other assurance providers	3	2	6				
Total effectiveness score	+K+L	+M+N	21	35	0.60		

Total overall score	Size score	X Control score	X Effectiveness score	0.185	200		37.00

Figure 4.10   Audit risk assessment model: network security (2)

5 *Undertaking a Risk-based Audit*

Risk-based assignment planning

Having determined a schedule of audit priorities and a plan of the assignments to be completed for the next year, the risk-based approach needs to be applied to the individual assignments.

Planning assignments carefully and effectively will save considerable time and effort during the audit itself. To quote Sir John Harvey-Jones, the famous business trouble shooter, 'Planning is an unnatural process; it is much more fun just to do something. And the nicest thing about not planning is that failure comes as a complete surprise, rather than being preceded by a period of worry and depression'. Fortunately auditors tend to be good at planning, so failure can be avoided.

Establishing the assignment plan

Effective planning is the route to success. The more prepared you are prior to commencing the audit work, the easier the actual assignment will be and the better the results.

Planning should ideally begin six to eight weeks prior to the scheduled start date for the assignment. The following template (Table 5.1) provides a good guide:

Table 5.1   Assignment planning

	✓ Date

1   Determine who, if anyone, will be working with the lead auditor on the assignment.
2   If so, arrange a short meeting with him/her to brainstorm the assignment.
3   Research the unit/topic via:
    • Intranet
    • Previous IA reports
    • Other assurance providers' reports (inc. External Audit)
    • Management reports
    • Statistics and trends
    • Risk analysis (if any)
    • Note down particular changes in structure, approach, management, and so on.
4 Brainstorm the risks by reference to the functional objectives (obtained hopefully by the research).	

5   Create a working paper file and index on the shared drive.
6   Contact the key customer for the assignment to arrange a pre-meeting.
7   Prepare the pre-meeting schedule.
8   Determine the main sources of information for the assignment by brainstorm and so on, and reference to last times' audit file (if there is one). This can then be incorporated in the scope and objectives memo.
9   Hold the pre-meeting to explain the audit, confirm functional objectives, discuss risks and determine scope and objectives of the assignment. Particular attention should be paid to concerns expressed by management regarding the audit area and additional aspects they would like to see covered. Do not adhere to such requests without considering the consequences (impact on plan, additional level of work required and so on). If you are in any doubt, refer to your manager before committing the department. If management request that the audit be postponed or topics or activities excluded, be very careful. Unless there is a very clear reason (other, therefore, than inconvenience, and so on) you should refer to your manager and revert back with the decision. Record all issues on the pre-meeting schedule.
10 Prepare scope and objectives memo. This should be issued to the manager with whom the pre-meeting was held (by e-mail). The manager should be encouraged to circulate the memo to relevant personnel within the areas to be covered by this audit. A covering letter/signature of acceptance is not required.
11 Prepare the control objectives schedule.
12 Arrange travel, visa, and so on.
13 Consider the interpersonal and cultural issues that may be encountered (particularly if this is your first visit to a particular country).
14 Assemble a working paper file to include all of the above plus:
    • Pre-audit PowerPoint presentation
    • FAQs schedule
    • Report template.

ALLOCATION OF AUDIT PERSONNEL

There is a great deal of debate regarding the benefits and drawbacks of resourcing audit assignments. Is it better to have auditors working alone? Or, assuming there are sufficient personnel, is it better to complete the assignment in pairs or indeed by a team of three or more.

My own experience suggests the following:

• If an auditor is new (less than six months in the role) it is better for him or her to jointly complete the audit assignment with a more experienced auditor.
• If the assignment is abroad it is more effective to send two auditors on the audit as they will have company and support; often critical in foreign parts.
• For all other assignments, I believe it is often more efficient to have auditors work alone (with periodic visits by a manager if the assignment time is longer than 10 to 14 days). The only exception should, in my view, be if the audit would take three weeks or more to finish on a single-handed basis.

I appreciate that not everyone will agree with this evaluation; it is important that you make your own judgements by reference to the complexity of both your organisation and the audits themselves.

Whatever conclusions you come to, one of the clear benefits of 'double heading' an assignment is that the two auditors can get together and brainstorm the audit at the planning stage which takes place typically six to eight weeks prior to commencing the fieldwork.

For single-handed assignments it is therefore very sensible for the auditor to sit down with a colleague (often his or her manager) to carry out this 'brainstorming'.

RESEARCHING THE AUDIT TOPIC

Many sources of information are available to the modern auditor at the planning stage:

- The Intranet can provide a very useful source of information, particularly if this is a new area for audit attention and background information is necessary.
- The previous audit reports (the last two) should always be referred to, particularly regarding recurrent failures to implement actions agreed or reluctance to accept recommendations made. This will help you to build a picture of the risk and control awareness and the attitude of management towards audit observations. Follow up reports (if available) provide another useful source of information.
- An area of attention that can pay significant dividends is to gather information about the management of the area being audited.
  - What has their attitude to auditors been in the past?
  - Have they been supportive or very difficult to deal with?
  - Are they team players or do they insist on always taking all the decisions?
  - What is their management style? Are they more interested in the big picture or the detail?
  - Will they insist on looking at all the angles before making a decision?
  - Will they need lots of evidence or will they recognise process opportunities without the need for detailed explanation?

Learning as much as possible about the key audit customers will give you enormous help in both audit interviews and the clearance meeting.

Other assurance providers' reports

These reports can come from the Compliance function, Health & Safety, the Risk Management function, External Audit or Quality Assurance. The more information you can glean from other independent reviews (and the issues uncovered) the better; it will help you build a picture of the area being audited even if you have no intention of covering the same areas as covered by the other assurance providers.

Statistics and trends

One of the most important developments in modern Internal Audit has been the emphasis on analytical review. Reviewing the key information concerning the function such as key financials, business performance and new developments provides the opportunity to build a picture of key trends. Armed with this information the areas of unusual experience or unexpected trends can be targeted during the audit.

Risk analysis

If there has been a self-assessment of the inherent and residual risks in the area under review, this analysis should also be examined, particularly the record of controls recorded.

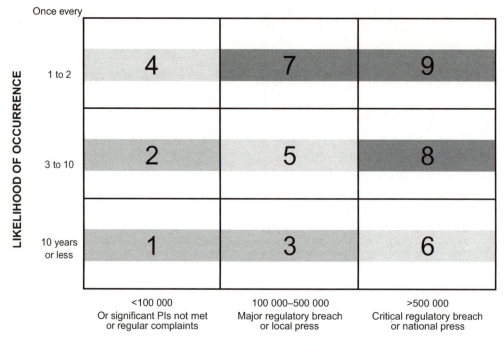

IMPACT ON BUSINESS

Figure 5.1   Risk assessment matrix

Particular attention should be given in the audit to risks where the inherent and residual risks are assessed as being markedly different, for example, inherent risks in Box 9 of the matrix and residual is Box 2.

Changes in structure, management and staff
A particularly important element of the planning phase is to determine any significant changes in personnel systems or procedure. The more changes there have been and the more significant these are, the more testing will be necessary.

Brainstorm the risks
This will be discussed in depth in the next section of this chapter: Determining the functional objectives.

CREATE A WORKING PAPER FILE

It is important that a file for the assignment is generated with easy reference to all who need it.

Audit working paper file contents
The audit file should always be in the same format. The best practice format below could be used.

- index
- audit report

- clearance meeting notes
- assignment plan
- audit assignment checklist
- audit classification
- research
- description of operations
- financial analysis
- audit history (previous reports, summaries, and so on)
- systems and processes
- other assurance reports (including External Audit)
- risk analysis (if available)
- key points of interest (unusual trends, changes since last review, and so on)
- sources of information
- pre-meeting notes
- scope and objectives memo
- audit programmes
- audit interviews
- control objectives and testing schedule
- personal learning record
- audit effectiveness questionnaire.

It is also very useful to develop an audit assignment checklist.

AUDIT ASSIGNMENT CHECKLIST

This checklist (Table 5.2) should help you to manage the audit effectively. Complete this schedule as you progress – it is organised in chronological order.

Table 5.2   Audit assignment checklist

	✓ Date
1 Introduce yourself to the key personnel.	
2 Ask for 15 minutes to explain the audit process – use the pre-audit PowerPoint as the basis.	
3 Confirm that personnel you need to speak to will actually be available and arrange specific times and dates for interviews.	
4 Complete the audit file in the format as per the audit checklist.	
5 Carry out interviews and complete interview record.	
6 Refine the audit programme as necessary.	
7 Prepare control objectives schedule.	
8 Determine audit test plan.	
9 Determine the level of testing required – check with the audit manager if you are in any doubt.	
10 Carry out walk-through tests (following a small number of transactions through the whole process) and record on the audit test schedule.	
11 Carry out other audit tests and record on the audit test schedule.	

12 Consider issues emerging and discuss findings with your manager – if further testing is required as a result complete this work and record as before.
13 Arrange clearance meeting – involve manager if you believe there are likely to be contentious issues.
14 Prepare for clearance meeting.
15 Determine and record audit classification – check this evaluation with your manager if there is any doubt at all.
16 Hold clearance meeting and record agreed actions and so on.
17 Prepare draft report.
18 Issue draft.
19 Discuss draft with management if necessary – incorporate management comments and update report if required.
20 Prepare and issue final report.
21 Determine audit effectiveness via a questionnaire.
22 Agree follow up date – and agree follow up process with management.

CONTACT THE KEY AUDIT CUSTOMER

You need to arrange a pre-meeting with the manager of the function you will be auditing. This meeting should ideally be held four weeks or so prior to the commencement of the fieldwork. It may, of course, not be practical to hold a face-to-face meeting if the location is in another country or a significant distance away from your base.

PRE-MEETINGS

A pre-meeting schedule should be used to record the key issues in the meeting with the functional manager.

An example of this pre-meeting schedule is reproduced in The Risk-based Auditing Toolkit, Section 12 (see Appendix).

SCOPE AND OBJECTIVES MEMO

The scope and objectives memo should be issued immediately after the pre-meeting with management, approximately four weeks before the start of the audit. This document represents the 'contract' between Internal Audit and management.

* Audit objectives
  Relate directly to the functional objectives, for example, to evaluate the effectiveness and efficiency of the raw materials procurement processes, and to ensure that all risks are being appropriately managed.
* Audit scope
  Detail the areas where the audit attention will be focused. Specifically refer to areas that will not be covered.
* Principal contacts
  The main contacts for the assignment are expected to be person A at location B.
* Information to have available
  Specify the main information and documents and records you will need to refer to during the audit.

- Audit duration
  X days with Z days on site beginning dd/mm/yy.
- Timetable
  Draft report expected dd/mm/yy.
- Audit team
  Names of auditors involved.

More information can be added in if you wish, such as the expected finish date on site. Some Internal Audit functions are keen to have the memo signed off by the audit customer. I believe that this is unnecessary; it might lead to resentment or mistrust on behalf of the functional manager involved.

CONTROL AND OBJECTIVES MEMO

The approach adopted varies considerably from Internal Audit function to Internal Audit function but it is generally agreed that a control objectives approach is a good one. This ensures that the risks, controls and audit tests carried out to evaluate them are recorded in a simple, cross-referenced manner.

An example of a controls objectives questionnaire is included in the Toolkit, Section 13 (see Appendix).

Determining the functional objectives

The key to effective risk-based assignment planning is to begin with the functional objectives, that is, the objectives of the system, activity or process that you are planning to review.

The best way to do so is to brainstorm and record the objectives yourself at the planning stage. These can then be shared with the functional manager at the pre-meeting. This will also demonstrate that you have given the audit some careful consideration and will provide a platform for the expert in the area, the manager in charge, an opportunity to add in any other objectives from his or her perspective.

To illustrate the process, consider an audit of Human Resources, one of the broader audit areas but one which is common to all organisations. The objectives will vary dependent on the specific responsibility of the Human Resources function but typically will include:

1 Ensure the organisation has the number and quality of staff to support its corporate objectives.
2 Maintain accurate and comprehensive personnel records for each employee.
3 Ensure all necessary information is obtained for employees, for example, references for new employees.
4 Ensure that the salary and benefits package is competitive.
5 Manage the job evaluation and grading structure for the business and ensure that these are compatible with the marketplace.
6 Establish and manage the sickness and absence policy.
7 Maintain overall holiday records for employees.
8 Establish and oversee the disciplinary and grievance procedures.

9 Represent the organisation in industrial tribunals, and so on.
10 Establish the process for exit interviews for leavers.
11 Ensure staff welfare.
12 Ensure that all employment regulations are complied with, for example, equal opportunities and data protection.
13 Co-ordinate training needs assessment and manage the overall training programme.
14 Ensure Human Resources and payroll records are synchronised.
15 Ensure all data is secure and backed up.
16 Ensure only authorised personnel can access the Human Resources system.

In this way, a very good picture of the function can be built up which may well highlight areas that otherwise would not be subject to audit. This is a particularly useful exercise for functions that have been audited many times before, as it may identify areas that have been omitted or not been looked at before.

Building a picture of the risks

The next step, having identified the objectives of the function, is to record the associated risks.

Whilst risks may have been identified formally during the CRSA programme, it is unlikely that the risk register will have recorded the risks at the detailed level required for audit purposes. It is therefore sensible to continue the brainstorming session by discussing and recording the associated risks. The whole process of brainstorming objectives and risks may take as little as 30 minutes and is well worth it in the context of an overall audit.

To continue the Human Resources audit example, the risks will include:

1 Inability to attract the necessary talent for the business.
2 Loss of key personnel.
3 Successful claims for unfair dismissal.
4 Inequality in job grading leading to bitterness.
5 Salary and benefits packages not in tune with the market.
6 Lack of key skills to meet business growth objectives.
7 New employees providing false information about previous employment or qualifications.
8 Regulatory breaches.
9 Fraudulent personnel records.
10 Excessive sickness or absence levels.
11 Hacking into the Human Resources database.
12 Loss of key information.
13 Unco-ordinated training programme.
14 Lack of staff to provide effective staff welfare.
15 Human Resources and payroll records not in agreement.
16 Uncontrolled holiday records.

Such a record (when complete) will provide an excellent template for the audit; if you can pose the question to management 'How are each of these individual risks managed?' you can establish clear control objectives which can then be evaluated by means of testing.

Determining the level of testing required

There are essentially two types of assignment – a review and an audit.

A review is an evaluation of a location or functional area carried out by the auditor by means of interviews with key personnel. Feedback is taken at face value and little testing is undertaken to confirm the accuracy of the information given. Little testing in this regard signifies a walk-through test or analytical review only.

An audit on the other hand builds on the information obtained from a review (as above) and employs techniques to systematically test samples or complete populations of data to provide firm evidence (normally statistically significant) regarding the successful (or otherwise) performance of controls and management of risk.

The decision whether to carry out a review or audit (and the depth and extent of resultant testing) will be determined by the following criteria:

1   The significance of the area to the business.
2   The inherent risks and their significance.
3   Concerns expressed.
4   Results of previous assurance reviews.
5   Results of meetings with management (issues highlighted, inconsistencies, and so on).
6   Extent of unusual trends, and so on.
7   Results of walk-through tests.
8   Obtaining sufficient evidence to convince management of the need for action.

Where it has been decided to carry out testing the following issues should be taken into account. If you are in any doubt consult your manager.

- Walk-through tests should always be completed.
- The greater the importance of the area to the business the more important it is to provide hard evidence.
- The greater the residual risk assessed the more evidence is required to ensure exposures are being managed effectively.
- Specific areas of concern expressed should be examined by transaction testing.
- Unusual trends uncovered should always be investigated.
- Any differences between actual and perceived controls observed during the walk-through tests should be investigated by means of transaction testing (5–10 items for a minor difference; 15–20 for a more fundamental discrepancy).
- Recurring issues from other audits and reviews should be given particular attention (if significant to the business objectives. You should not, however, duplicate work carried out recently (that is, within the last six months) – but rely on those results).

Methods of testing

The following methods of testing are the main ones to be used. Determine the appropriate approach in discussion with your manager.

Analytical review is carried out at overview level and includes comparing recorded information to that expected, budgeted or achieved in past periods. This technique is used as a 'reality check' on the system of control to ensure that the system is operating effectively in a macro sense. Unexpected variances are identified and investigated to understand how they have arisen. It is best to perform analytical reviews during the earliest stage of an audit to identify areas of concern and direct work accordingly.

Interviewing is the asking of questions to a knowledgeable person, listening to and evaluating the response, asking appropriate follow-up questions and obtaining corroborating information as appropriate. Corroborating evidence from individuals independent of the respondent represents a higher quality of evidence. The review should be fully documented.

Observation is watching a procedure being performed. Observation provides strong evidence covering the time an event is performed and can yield indicators about the level of knowledge of the person performing the action, but it is not in itself indicative of consistency or performance of the act in other periods.

Walk-through tests involve following the processing of a limited sample of data through the whole system. They will serve to confirm understanding of the processes being operated and provide some evidence (although not a statistically valid sample) of the actual operation of controls.

Population audit is the searching of a whole population for items that have a defined specific characteristic or to compare two or more fields or files. A population audit is an evaluation of a full population of data or a subset of the whole in order to confirm the validity of all transactions (or attributes thereof). Such samples should be based on achieving maximum financial coverage with minimal sample size (the 80/20 rule).

Transaction testing or compliance testing is the evaluation of a sample of the population for compliance with the stated controls. The purpose of the test is to confirm that the transactions under review were subjected to the controls specified at the time of the review as well as to test the level of documentation, or audit trail, created.

AUDIT AS A CATALYST FOR CHANGE

Whilst the primary role of Internal Audit is to assist management in the effective discharge of their duties by objectively evaluating the effectiveness of systems, procedures and processes in place it is increasingly recognised that there is an opportunity to take a much more proactive role.

As Internal Audit have a wide remit and often a unique insight into the disciplines in place, as a result of their independence and wide knowledge of the business, they will often be in a position to identify inefficient processes, unnecessary or over-engineered controls and offer fresh insight, challenges and alternatives to enable management to reassess the current approaches.

In this way audit can act as a catalyst for change.

Look for such areas of opportunity in every assignment. Ask yourself:

- Is there another way to achieve the same result with less effort or less cost?
- What duplication or apparent duplication is there?
- When was the last time the processes were reviewed by management?
- What changes were made?
- How effective have they been?

Dealing with audit customers

The important thing to remember in your audit work is to deal with the customers in a professional and courteous way:

- Treat them with respect; they are the experts in their function and you are entering their territory.
- Answer all questions calmly and in a matter of fact way even if the customer is abrasive or even aggressive towards you.
- Make sure you are open to ideas. If the functional manager identifies the appropriate solution he or she is much more likely to implement it, than if you suggested the same solution.
- Ensure management appreciate that you are carrying out the audit for their benefit (not your own).
- Ask them who they would suggest you interview and ensure that they will be there during the audit. This might seem obvious but it is most annoying and very inefficient in terms of the audit if, say, two of the four key personnel are not there when you arrive to commence the assignment.
- Preparing a schedule of the personnel to interview may be a good idea, particularly if the audit is a complex one and needs to be co-ordinated.
- Interviews should be brief; thirty minutes or so is ideal.
- Interview senior management first to get their perspective (as they may have information about imminent changes, and so on)
- Then interview the owners of the key data and finally the staff (if you need to understand the detailed procedures).
- The key to success in audit interviews is to let the customer do most of the talking; you are trying to build up the most comprehensive picture you can.
- Ask about changes since the last audit rather than asking for a full description of the document flows, and so on, as this only annoys the customer. They will quite rightly tend to ask why you have not got a record of the procedures established during the previous review.
- Use mind mapping or other recognised techniques if you can to visually record the system or document flows. Mind mapping is akin to simple flowcharting and is an excellent technique for the modern auditor. For more information visit www.mind-map.com
- Ask about areas of concern but do not highlight any of your own, particularly to more senior functional management, as this may cause them to overreact or lead to a frantic desire to 'get to the bottom of the problem'; which often can cause unnecessary disruption or blame being apportioned without the full facts being known.

Audit programmes

Audit programmes have been largely replaced by the control objectives and testing schedules already referred to. Where audit programmes are used they tend to be much less rigid than in the past and are used more as skeletons rather than detailed 'to do lists'. They tend to be developed for the specific assignment unless the audits are repeated many times during the year, for example, branch audits and are developed in outline form to ensure that the auditors are forced to think rather than carry out the audit as automatons.

One of the best sources of skeleton audit programmes and many other audit related topics is the excellent website, www.auditnet.org. This free site is widely regarded as the leading Internal Audit site.

The use of audit tools

A variety of excellent Internal Audit software tools are available, all of which are designed to improve the efficiency and effectiveness of the audit. Amongst the computer-assisted audit techniques the most highly regarded are the two products referred to in Chapter 4, ACL and IDEA.

Both operate in a Windows environment and allow file comparisons, trends and other specific audit tests to be carried out on a copy of the files loaded onto a stand-alone PC. The tests which can be completed are only limited by your imagination. To get the most out of such packages you need to allocate an IT literate member of the audit staff to co-ordinate this aspect of the audit process, as some knowledge of the data and how it is organised is necessary to use the tools effectively.

The alternative is to use the functionality within your own system, particularly if your organisation uses SAP or a similar enterprise wide solution. The reporting capability built into these systems is comprehensive but, of course, they are not designed specifically with audit in mind. Many Internal Audit functions, however, use such tools very effectively for audit purposes.

The other tools used by Internal Auditors are those designed for planning and co-ordinating the audit process. It is fair to say that whilst these can be used by any Internal Audit function they yield the greater benefits to functions with 10+ staff.

The software varies considerably in specification and price but with the right amount of effort can be used to improve the consistency and efficiency of the audit management process.

The products which are most commonly used by the Internal Audit functions in The Business Risk Management Ltd database of 3000 audit functions are (in no particular order):

Horwath's Galileo package – www.horwath.com
Methodware's Planning Advisor & Pro Audit Advisor – www.methodware.com
Pentana's PAWS Audit & Risk management software – www.pentana.com
PWC's Teammate package – www.pwc.com
JE Boritz's Audit Masterplan package – www.jebcl.com

Determining the threats to success

The final aspect of risk-based assignment planning is to consider the threats or risks to success of the audit and how these should be addressed. Amongst the risks to the audit are:

- You might not be able to complete the audit within the time allotted.
- The management or staff of the function being reviewed may be obstructive.
- You may find the audit requires more technical or functional specific knowledge than you anticipated.
- The attitude of the management may change during the assignment if you identify areas which they believe are weaknesses.
- There may be a clash of personalities between one or more auditors and the functional management.
- You may find nothing to report on.
- You may miss major issues such as possible fraud.

Let us look at each risk in turn:

NOT BEING ABLE TO COMPLETE THE AUDIT TO TIME

This can be due to a number of reasons including the inexperience of the auditor, identifying areas of poor control which need to be reviewed in more depth and the need to re-perform tasks or gain more evidence after audit management review. The inexperience issue should be easy to predict and the risk can be mitigated by having a new auditor accompanied by a more experienced colleague. However, the more likely problem area is when an inexperienced auditor is given his or her first few solo assignments. For these audits it is a very good idea to send along the manager or a senior colleague at two or three key stages in the audit (depending of course on the overall duration of the assignment). This will ensure that, if difficulties are arising or timescales are likely not to be met, action can be taken, such as sending another auditor to assist.

The key in all such cases is to try to complete the audit in the elapsed time notified to management or explain to them why this is not possible. If you have agreed to spend two weeks on site and you are there for three, this will be a major negative issue for functional management. The only real valid reason for an extension should be that many risk and control opportunities have been identified and to be able to add the greatest value, it was necessary to assess the issues in more depth than would normally have been necessary.

MANAGEMENT OR STAFF BEING OBSTRUCTIVE

I am sure that most Internal Auditors will have encountered this problem. Being obstructive can manifest itself in many ways:

- only answering direct questions;
- only giving the most cursory of answers to questions;
- denying access to information or documentation;
- holding back key information;

- deliberately avoiding the auditor by being off site at key stages or during the whole audit;
- not providing the information when asked for it, for example, failing to get the documents from the archives after providing assurances that they would be obtained;
- telling staff to give no support.

There are many ways of spotting when you are not being given the full picture.

Mike Comer's book *Deception at Work: Investigating and Countering Lies and Fraud Strategies* (Michael J. Comer and Timothy E. Stephens, Gower Publishing, 2004) provides excellent guidance on this subject.

The way to deal with deliberately obstructive personnel is to be firm, professional and to explain the need for information and, if necessary, the right of access you have to any information, using the relevant section of the audit charter if you feel this will help.

Where only direct questions are being answered continue to ask more questions until you hopefully get the information you need. Press for detail if only cursory answers are being given or ask the same questions of other managers/staff and compare the responses.

Denying access to documents is probably the most awkward situation. Whilst you have the right to see any documents you wish, as per your charter, if the customer believes that the information is very sensitive it may be advisable to show your understanding of this sensitivity by the documents being provided only to senior audit management. This is a good way of defusing a potentially explosive situation.

If a key contact is being deliberately unavailable (or you suspect they are not wanting to see you) the best approach is to inform that person, by telephone message or e-mail, that you will therefore have to deal with the team members and that more disruption will be necessary as a result. This will usually do the trick!

THE AUDIT REQUIRES MORE TECHNICAL OR BUSINESS KNOWLEDGE THAN YOU EXPECTED

The planning phase, if carried out in sufficient depth, should have alerted you to these pitfalls. However, problems can occur if the audit customer tries, for example, to make the auditor uneasy by asking questions such as:

- 'What do you know about this area, have you ever worked in IT?'
- 'Do you think that the SLA for the DPS will provide the RMC with the NAR?' that is, trying deliberately to baffle you with jargon.

Clearly, if it transpires that real technical knowledge is required, you might need to draft in additional expertise to the assignment. Explaining that you are focusing on the process rather than technical details of the system itself will usually diffuse another potentially awkward situation, particularly if you massage the assailant's ego regarding their expertise regarding such technical aspects.

The intent to baffle with jargon is a simple one to deal with. Explain you cannot be an expert in all functions of the organisation and ask for an explanation of each acronym.

CLASH OF PERSONALITIES

Despite all best efforts there are some occasions where auditors and management do not see eye to eye. You will certainly be notified of this conflict if you are the manager responsible for the auditor, usually with an accompanying request such as 'Please do not send him again'.

The usual reason for such a clash is that the personalities are very similar, for example, two egotists will not usually get on well together.

You can foresee such clashes if you know enough about the key audit customer and the styles of your audit team members. It may not be wise to send your staff into assignments where such altercations could occur, but you will need to be diplomatic when explaining the reasons to the auditors involved.

A better solution is to take the time to train your team members to deal with personnel who have either a very similar style or a dramatically different one.

A number of different methods and techniques can be used to assess personality traits and success drivers, the method which I prefer is the Honey and Mumford one which is based on learning styles and personal drivers (see Table 5.3).

Explanation of the Four Learning Styles

ACTIVISTS

Activists involve themselves fully with great fervour in any new experiences. They enjoy the

Table 5.3   Influence with impact: Honey and Mumford's learning styles

Activists	*Reflectors*
• Try anything once • Enjoy fire-fighting • Get bored with following things through • Like to work with others	• Like to stand back and look in • Analyse information carefully before coming to conclusions • Consider all factors before making a decision • Act with caution • Observe others carefully
Theorists	*Pragmatists*
• Enjoy theories, models and lateral thinking • Logical and rational • Enjoy analysis and evaluation • Do not like things to be too subjective • Try to fit ideas into their own theories	• Love new situations and techniques • Like to apply new ideas to their environment • Recognise what is practical and what is not • Do not have problems – only challenges and opportunities • Need clear goals and objectives

Source: *Learning Styles Questionnaire*, Peter Honey and Alan Mumford, Peter Honey Publishing (1992). For more information: www.peterhoney.com

present and are happy with immediate experiences. They are open-minded and very enthusiastic about anything new. Their philosophy is 'I'll try anything once'. They tend to act first and consider the implications later. They are very busy people. They enjoy brainstorming. As soon as the excitement from one activity has subsided they are busy looking for the next challenge. They get bored easily, so they often fail to follow things through to a conclusion. They are very sociable people, constantly involving themselves with others, but in doing so they like to be the centre of attention.

REFLECTORS

Reflectors like to stand back to consider experiences and observe them from many different perspectives. They collect a great deal of information and prefer to consider everything thoroughly before coming to any conclusion. The careful collection and analysis of data is critical to a reflector, so they tend to put off decisions for as long as possible. They tend to be very cautious and thoughtful people. They prefer to take a secondary role in meetings and discussions, but when they do get involved their contributions tend to be very incisive. They enjoy watching others and how they react to different situations. They tend to adopt a low profile and sometimes may be regarded as aloof or haughty. They are not easily annoyed and are excellent team players. When they act it is usually for the common good and the ideas will be very well thought through.

THEORISTS

Theorists like to fit problems, ideas and indeed the world into their own theories. They are very logical and analytical thinkers assessing problems in a very structured and rational manner. They are able to assimilate a great deal of conflicting information and make sense of it. They tend to be very tidy-minded and can be seen as perfectionists or even zealots who won't be happy until everything fits into 'boxes'. They love making or hearing about others' assumptions and principles. They are excellent at understanding systems and complex processes. They cannot easily understand why everyone does not think like they do. They tend to be very dedicated and loyal people and will always give an objective judgement. They like certainty and feel uncomfortable with subjective judgements and others who do not take business seriously.

PRAGMATISTS

Pragmatists love trying out new ideas and approaches to see if they work in practice. They search out new ideas and are often the first to experiment with new products or ideas. They are not fazed by failure – they regard it as part of the learning experience. 'Better to have tried and failed than not tried at all' could be their maxim. They like to act quickly and are very confident in their own abilities. They tend to be rather impatient people and like to come to clear conclusions. They are very practical and positive and see problems as opportunities. They take criticism as a learning opportunity. They are usually excellent problem-solvers. They recognise the bigger picture but also their own inadequacies.

If you can spot the different traits in a person you are dealing with, you can adapt to the situation to optimise the chance of success. This is particularly important in a clearance meeting with contentious issues to discuss.

Table 5.4   Influence with impact: Personal drivers

Success	Status
• Free of boundaries	• Needs to be respected
• Risk taker	• Very keen on personal image
• Results oriented	• Like to be in control
• Can see the bigger picture	• Wants to do things their way
• Opportunity taker	• They believe their way is right
	• They want to win even if others lose
Safety	*Social*
• Knows the right way to do something	• Needs to be liked
	• Wants to be accepted
• Keen on detail	• Hates conflict
• Recognises the benefit of clear procedures	• Tries to keep morale up
	• Equality and fairness are critical
• Believe 'if it is not broken – why fix it'	• Wants to be a team member
	• Works towards common goals
• Safety first focus	
• Not keen on taking risks	

Source: *Learning Styles Questionnaire* (Peter Honey and Alan Mumford, 1992).

If the manager of the function being audited, for example, is an activist they are not likely to be interested in a great deal of detail whereas a reflector is much more likely to ask questions about the evidence. Equally a manager with a strong status personal driver will want to determine the actions themselves to take rather than Internal Audit suggesting them.

Studying the traits and adapting to meet the style of the key personnel in the function under review will significantly enhance your chance of agreement and a positive reaction to the audit.

FINDING NOTHING TO REPORT

This may be a risk but in reality it should not be a concern. If the function is really well managed and there are only two or three minor issues, it is better to issue a one-page report identifying that the function is being effectively managed. Otherwise you will be accused of nitpicking.

MISSING CRITICAL ISSUES

This is one of the biggest concerns (and indeed terrors) faced by Internal Audit. 'What if we miss something and there is a huge problem in three months time?'

The good news is that the methodical process-driven risk-based approach is designed to assess all the key activities, risks and controls and therefore major areas of concern should be identified.

The bad news is that:

- If you have restricted the audit to specific areas of a function and the problems occur in the area not reviewed you may be accused of not looking at the critical areas. Creating a risk-based audit plan should ensure that this is a very uncommon occurrence but of course can still happen. You have to take some risk!
- Unless you use a computer-assisted audit tool, such as ACL or IDEA, you will only have been able to review a small number of transactions covering a relatively short period of time. You cannot therefore hope to identify everything. It is important that this is appreciated by management, hence the need to get them to determine the level of assurance they require as explained in Chapter 6.
- Fraud can often be perpetrated even with good controls in place, as the fraudster is often a senior member of staff (all the research and surveys carried out during the past five years confirms this) and can therefore get round the controls.

You need a different approach to tackle the threat of fraud. The following list of fraud indicators should form part of the auditor's toolkit.

FRAUD INDICATORS

Behaviours

- dramatic changes in lifestyle (driving a new Ferrari or bragging about the new Rolex watch);
- extravagant spending, for example, gifts for staff;
- no holidays taken;
- inappropriate lifestyle for the job;
- rumours spread regularly by one person;
- regular rumours about a person;
- sudden increase in backlog of work;
- number of hours worked suddenly rockets;
- someone working very late on a regular basis;
- the person becomes a hermit;
- signs of unusual stress;
- sudden antagonism;
- obsessive bureaucracy – where the person used not to be;
- people being too co-operative – all of a sudden;
- stubborn unwillingness to enhance controls;
- concentration of responsibility – taking on work usually delegated;
- unwillingness to meet face to face;
- personnel who initiate actions without approval – with a series of excuses.

Results

- results buck the trend;
- always just meets budget;
- unexpectedly consistent results;
- always reports results early;
- erratic performance;
- unusual volume of cash transactions;
- bad debt write offs – outside normal limits.

Documentation

- 'lost' documentation;
- erased or crossed out figures;
- post dated cheques;
- unusual fonts – for example, different from those expected in internal documents;
- altered figures after document authorised;
- missing sequences;
- non serial numbered transactions;
- same distinct style or format in documents from apparently unconnected sources;
- regular round sum transactions;
- many transactions for exactly the same sum;
- values consistently just below authorisation limits;
- high level of credit notes;
- absence of supporting documentation;
- same payee addresses for apparently unconnected people.

Relationships

- domineering individuals;
- unusual business structures;
- very regular visits by same customers, and so on;
- noticeable hospitality;
- unusual terms and conditions in agreements;
- unrealistic prices;
- claims outside normal levels;
- unusual turnover of staff;
- unusual level of staff loans;
- customer anomalies – same names appearing regularly;
- concerted attempts to postpone management visits;
- unusual volume of loans to employees;
- use of fronts – alter egos, name variations to conceal conflicts of interest.

Risk-based auditing is a process, a rationale, even a philosophy but it cannot insulate you against all eventualities. Remember auditing itself is a risky business.

6 *Risk-based Audit Reporting*

Objectives of reporting

The audit report is arguably the most important aspect of the whole audit process. You can have chosen the right topic, evaluated the results effectively, assessed the controls in depth, and recorded the results in an elegantly produced cross reference working paper but, if the report does not reflect this excellence, you will not be seen to have succeeded. After all the report is probably the only product that the management of the function being audited will see.

The report therefore needs to be treated like gold and the report itself as the shining jewel in your shop window.

WHAT ARE THE OBJECTIVES OF THE REPORT?

1   To reflect the observations from the audit in a professional manner.
2   To give an appropriate level of assurance commensurate with those observations.
3   To make recommendations for improving risk management and controls.
4   To identify over-managed areas and unnecessary controls.
5   To advise on the practical balance between risk and control.

Who is the report for?

The recipients of the report are, typically, senior management, local management (of the functions being audited), the Audit Committee, External Audit and possibly regulatory bodies. The difficulty is that each of these parties wants something quite different, but you have to satisfy them all in the same report. This is a tall order and is perhaps one of the reasons why writing Internal Audit reports is not at all easy and why the risk-based approach needs to be extended into the report itself.

The need for reports with impact

Imagine that you are at the airport, just about to travel away to some exotic location for a holiday. You decide to browse through the bookshop to select a book or two to enjoy whilst you are away. How do you decide which book to buy? If you think about it, you first have to decide which book to pick up to examine. This is likely to be because:

• you like books by a particular author and have searched out one you have not read, or

- the cover of the book is enticing (with an image that grabs your attention or strong colours), or
- the book has been displayed in an interesting way, for example, full face rather than end on or on a pile with others described as bestsellers, and so on.

Having decided to pick the book up, whatever your motivation to do so, what do you do next?

It is likely that you read the critiques of the book on the back or inside covers, this still appears strange to me (although I do it as well) for have you ever seen a critique that says 'This book is awful, don't buy it' printed on the book? No, they only ever praise it.

The next action you probably take is to read the blurb of the book, usually on the first page or inside jacket flap and, if this interests you, the next stage will be to read the first paragraph of the book itself.

Does this sound familiar? You will therefore probably have chosen a book, or indeed many, on the basis of the look of the front cover, a few words attributed by a reviewer of the book and reading the first paragraph.

The reality is that audit reports are no different. Most of the impact of the audit report needs to be made in the first thirty seconds or so after the report is picked up or looked at on a computer screen.

Creating an enticing front page and having a clear attention-grabbing executive summary are the keys to success.

Just think about the mountain of correspondence, reports and emails that you receive in a week. Which of them do you read immediately and which do you put to one side either physically or mentally to read later?

The question is do you want your audit reports to be put in the 'read later' pile. I am sure that you do not.

If you want your reports dealt with quickly they need to be attention grabbing. Does your Internal Audit function use colour in its reports? Those that do inform us of a significant improvement in the reaction to them and in the proportion of recommendations implemented.

What makes a good report?

Our research of directors reveals the following factors that separate an excellent Internal Audit from one that is not so good.

- *Timeliness* is regarded as particularly important. If it takes two months to finalise the report, by the time the Director responsible receives it, the importance of the issues and the impact will be lost.
- *Relevance* to the recipient is also seen as very important. Directors are very busy people and if they receive a report which they regard as unimportant or not related to their area of focus you will not be thanked.
- *Accuracy* is paramount. If you get just one fact wrong in the report, the whole report can often be called into question by the recipients.
- *Focused*: management want the report to get straight to the point, be organised in order of importance and not include unnecessary information.

- *Brevity* is probably one of the most significant differences between the excellent report and the 'also ran'. Brevity is not just about how many pages there are in the report, although this is a crucial issue, it is also about using as few words as possible, short paragraphs, and so on.
- *Clarity* is also a major factor. A well formatted and clearly laid out report is much easier to read, understand and respond to.
- Reports should be *unambiguous*. The reader should not be left wondering what you were trying to say or include contradictions or vague generalisations.
- Above all the reports should be very *simple to follow*; the more senior the recipient the simpler it needs to be. This is because such executives are very busy and will not have the time to work out what you were trying to say. Simple to follow also includes the need for simple language, sitting with a thesaurus to find the most complex word you can might seem a nice idea but if the recipient has to then look up the meaning, you will not have succeeded. Keeping the report as simple as possible is particularly good advice if you are required to write the report in a language that is not your mother tongue.
- *Jargon-free* reports should definitely be the aim. Whilst local management may well understand the abbreviations and three letter acronyms, it is much less likely that the Board and, indeed, the Audit Committee will do so. If you must put in abbreviations, explain the meaning the first time you use them.
- *Avoid waffling* or padding the report unnecessarily. Management of the function being audited know the procedures in depth. Long explanations of what you did or in-depth descriptions of the system and all its processes are not necessary.
- *Clear conclusions* are crucial. You need to ensure that the reader understands exactly what you think about the efficiency and effectiveness of the activity under review. A clearly stated audit opinion is the best way to achieve this goal.
- *Practical recommendations* are regarded as a vital ingredient of a good report. If the recommendations you are making are not capable of implementation, the question that needs to be asked is 'Why are you making them?'
- The final key issue highlighted by senior management is the need to have *agreed actions* in the report. If you leave the report open with a series of recommendations, senior management then have to take the time to determine the actions that will be taken. If you specify the actions that have been agreed and the timescales for their introductions, senior management do not have to guess the outcome.

Each of these key elements will be discussed in more depth later.

Forty questions about reports

A good way to assess the effectiveness and quality of your audit report is to answer the following forty questions which relate to reports issued in the last 12 months. Each question represents best practice and the rationale for each activity or measure is explained in the next part of the book.

Table 6.1   Forty questions about reports

	Yes/No
1 Have more than 95 per cent of audit recommendations been fully and successfully implemented?	
2 Did your report refer to the organisation's objectives and how the audit recommendations would assist?	
3 Were all reports six pages or less?	
4 Did the reports take less than two weeks to finalise from the end of the fieldwork to the final report?	
5 Were all observations and recommendations different from the last time an audit of the area was carried out?	
6 Did the reports include graphics (charts, diagrams, and so on)?	
7 Did the reports include photos where appropriate?	
8 Were they issued electronically?	
9 Were all issues fully discussed before the reports were issued, that is, no surprises?	
10 Did the reports focus on the future rather than the past?	
11 Did management comments indicate real commitment rather than a way for the customer to close the process and get rid of you?	
12 Did you give a specific audit opinion?	
13 Did the customer accept this opinion as valid?	
14 Did the observations, conclusions and recommendations really represent the key issues?	
15 Do you only report on the major issues, with the minor ones being dealt with separately?	
16 Were all recommendations 100 per cent practical?	
17 Were the audits conducted recognised by the organisation as helpful and relating to key risks or opportunities?	
18 Were the reports a true reflection of the expertise and knowledge that went into the audits?	
19 Have you had positive unsolicited comments about the value added by more than three audits in the last 12 months?	
20 Did you quantify the cost/benefit of each audit?	
21 Was this published on the face of the report?	
22 Did your final reports incorporate agreed actions rather than recommendations?	
23 Were named owners included for each action?	
24 Were firm implementation dates committed to?	
25 Were more than 80 per cent of the agreed actions/recommendations implemented within the time scale agreed?	
26 Did the reports have Executive Summaries?	
27 Were these issued in isolation (that is, without the main report) to senior management?	
28 Were reports posted on your Intranet pages?	
29 Was any other information relating to the audits posted on the Intranet, for example, terms of reference, best practice ideas, working papers?	
30 Were owners of actions of sufficient seniority to implement them without further approval?	
31 Are your reports jargon free?	

32   Do all reports have summarised action plans (typically together at the end of the report)?

33   Does the Audit Committee ask to see reports or a summary thereof?

34   Does the Chief Executive get to see all reports (Executive Summaries or full)?

35   Have you asked management formally, during the last 12 months, for their assessment of your audit report formats, quality, and so on?

36   Is this an annual process? How was this information gathered?

37   Have you changed the report formats significantly in the last two years?

38   If you were the recipient of the reports, would they have spurred you into action?

39   Have you avoided including any unnecessary background information in the reports?

40   Do you believe that your reports are as good as they could be?

Score 1 point for each 'Yes'.

How did you score?

0 – 10	You need a complete rethink of your audit report process.
11 – 20	Many opportunities for improving audit reporting.
21 – 30	Enough areas to get you thinking.
31 – 35	You have clearly put a great deal of effort into reporting.
36 – 40	Are you telling the truth?

IMPLEMENTATION OF RECOMMENDATIONS

If you can honestly say that more than 95 per cent of the audit recommendations have been successfully implemented, you are one of the top 10 per cent of audit functions in the world in this regard. The average is about 70–75 per cent.

A question: If the percentage implementation on average is around 75 per cent, does this mean that you have wasted 25 per cent of your effort?

This may seem a very harsh assessment, but you have only made a difference to the business with 75 per cent of the suggestions made; certainly senior management would probably see it that way.

If 95 per cent plus is best practice for implementation of recommendations, how can this be achieved? The issues highlighted in the other 39 questions provide the clues.

Do not congratulate yourself too soon if you have achieved 95 per cent successful implementation, if, for example, the remaining 5 per cent were the most critical recommendations.

REFERENCE TO BUSINESS OBJECTIVES

The risk-based approach highlighted in Chapter 5 predicates the determination of functional objectives. Referring to the objectives is an excellent way of gaining commitment and understanding.

BREVITY

The most successful Internal Audit functions are the ones that consistently produce short, sharp, focused reports. The six-page report, whilst a challenge for many Internal Audit functions is one of the best methods of creating impact and improving the implementation rate for recommendations made.

A short report is usually easier to write, easier to review, easier to read and easier to respond to – a win, win, win, win situation.

You may well be saying at this point that the report length will depend upon the number of issues that need to be raised and if the whole area is a shambles filling a six-page report may be totally impossible. I agree with you up to a point. I am taking the six-page report as an average, but I would find it hard to accept that there is ever justification for a report to be longer than 12 pages.

If I break down the six-page report into its key components, this hopefully will explain my assertion about maximum report length:

Cover page (if you need one).
Page 1   The Executive Summary (No contents page is necessary in a short report).
Pages 2–5   Main Report.
Page 6   Action Plan.

No appendices are necessary to be incorporated in the report; if you must have them, post them on the Intranet site, only a very few of the recipients will be interested in them.

The main report will therefore have four pages. If you cover the issues raised briefly (as you should), you should be able to cover three to four issues per page. Even in a short report therefore you can include 12 to 16 separate issues.

In a 12-page report with nine pages for the main report and two for the action plan, you can cover 27 to 36 issues. It is difficult to envisage needing to report on more than 30 major points.

REPORT FINALISATION

One of the biggest challenges facing Internal Audit functions is to finalise the report quickly. The best practice (that is, what the most successful Internal Audit functions are able to achieve) is less than two weeks from completion of the audit fieldwork to issuing the final report.

If this appears a step too far, by breaking down the steps and the reason for delay, it should be possible for most Internal Audit functions to reduce the elapsed time for issue of their reports.

Issue of the draft report

The average period between audit work completion and issue of the draft is seven to ten days. The very best functions achieve this task in one to two days.

How they do it is to write sections of the report as they progress during the assignment – creating a rough draft as they go along. The audit management tools invariably have a feature to facilitate this process.

A big advantage of this approach is that the rough draft can be available to give to the audit customer at the clearance meeting. Having something in writing is a huge bonus, as it is then much less likely that the recipient will argue with the words or the emphasis given to certain topics. As you will probably already know, a common source of tension and delay is that management do not like the wording used in the draft report as they argue it is not representative of the discussion at the clearance meeting.

The next step in the issue of the draft is the need for the report to be reviewed by the audit manager. A common source of delay is that the manager is not available on the day when the draft is ready for review.

It should not be difficult to plan this in advance. It will be known, usually with a good deal of accuracy, how long the audit will take. If the review process is planned in at the start of the assignment, the manager will be available and scheduled in; and the right amount of pressure will be applied on the auditor or auditors to complete the assignment on time.

For example, if the audit is due to start on Monday, 1 March for a duration of two weeks and one day is allocated for collation of the draft report, the manager will be scheduled to be available on Tuesday, 16 March to review the draft report and working papers.

The other reason for drafts not being issued in a sufficiently timely manner is often due to the manager's review process itself.

This is certainly a contentious area but however tempting it is to change the report wording, or have the auditor do so, it is much better to resist the temptation unless, of course:

- There are inaccuracies in the facts.
- The wording completely misrepresents the situation.
- The manager has knowledge of very recent changes in the area that the auditor could not have.

Changing the wording just because the manager would not have written it in that particular way is not justifiable and is very annoying to the auditor who has drafted the report. However, many audit managers think that if they make no changes, there was no purpose to the review. Change for the sake of change is no use to anybody.

The key is to keep the review process very structured and simple and not to seek perfection – you can never achieve it.

Under no circumstances should there be more than one draft of a report! If you have three to four drafts, as some Internal Audit functions do, look very carefully at the process and reduce the drafts one by one until you can achieve the whole review process in one sitting.

Some Internal Audit functions require two levels of review, for example, the audit manager and the Head of Internal Audit. These reviews can and should be carried out at the same time; otherwise you will find that alterations made by the manager are often changed again by the Head of Internal Audit on his or her review.

The Head of Internal Audit should, quite rightly, be given the opportunity to look at the report before issue, but in my view this should not be at the draft stage, but rather just before the final report is issued.

Issue of the final report

Whilst the issue of the draft report is totally under Internal Audit's control, the finalisation of the report is not, as it is dependent upon the recipients giving their comments and formal agreements.

There are, however, a number of ways in which you can facilitate a swift finalisation:

- Issuing the draft within two days of the audit completion will provide the impetus for a swift response. The issues will still be fresh in the minds of the managers. If it takes ten days to issue the draft, why should the recipient bother to respond within five days or less?

- For managers who you know will be slow to respond (and every organisation has such people) arrange a short meeting in their diary to get the management comments, and so on. Note that these personnel may not be the same ones who attend the clearance meeting. This meeting should be arranged at the start of the assignment rather than after issue of the draft. It is highly unlikely that you will be able to secure a meeting, however short, with key personnel at a few days' notice but will be able to do so a month in advance.
- Make it easy to respond by offering the opportunity to respond by e-mail or by phone call.
- Keep the wording of recommendations and agreements obtained at the clearance meeting simple and to the point.

REPORTING AUDIT OBSERVATIONS

If you are finding that the issues highlighted in reports were the same or similar to those raised when the audit was last completed, this is not a good reflection on the Internal Audit function. This signifies that you have not been able to convince management to implement the recommendations the first time.

In fact one of the more recent and perhaps contentious initiatives is to seriously consider abandoning the audit if it is clear on the first day or so that many of the areas of concern raised during the previous audit of the area still remain.

The argument for stopping the audit is that your time and resources are valuable and very limited and it is better to put the resources where they can achieve the most benefit; repeating the audit and highlighting the same issues all over again is clearly not a good use of the audit team.

Under these circumstances you should report to the Director or General Manager of the area under review and inform them that they should ensure that pressure is applied to address the concerns raised.

THE USE OF GRAPHICS

The use of graphics such as charts, diagrams and graphs is an excellent way of splitting up the text and making the report easier to read and understand. Try and use some form of graphic rather than tables of figures or long appendices. It is usually the trend that you are trying to highlight rather than the figures themselves.

THE USE OF PHOTOGRAPHS

The use of a carefully taken photo, taken by a digital camera, can be extremely powerful in an audit report. It is said that a picture is worth a thousand words.

If you are completing an audit of a physical area, such as a manufacturing area, stores or even an IT installation, take along a camera. Often the inclusion of a photo can capture action much better than a page of text.

I have seen situations where a key issue, which has been a problem for a long time because local management have been unable to convince senior management of its importance, has been resolved very quickly by the use of a photo in the report.

METHOD OF ISSUE

Hopefully most Internal Audit functions now issue their reports by electronic means. There is then no worry about printing reports or whether to bind them and there can be little argument about safe receipt.

The only concern that I have heard is that Word-based reports could be altered by the recipient. As you have the original authorised version, I do not believe that this is a valid concern. However, one of the most modern techniques is to issue the report as a PDF file, which eliminates this risk (or almost) as most people do not have the facilities to amend PDF files. I do think that PDF is an excellent format for audit reports and is worthy of consideration for all Internal Audit functions.

LACK OF SURPRISES

This should not be a problem for most audit functions. If management argue that all the issues were not fully discussed before the report was issued, then you are in a very awkward position. Most commonly, it transpires that the argument is about the extent of criticism rather than the issue itself. We will discuss this area in more detail later in the chapter.

The only time when real surprises do emerge is when the Director or senior management receive the report. Given that it is unlikely that they will have been involved during the discussion of the draft, there is always a chance that, due to information that they have but their local management do not, the action agreed could be countermanded or significantly changed.

This can be a difficult situation but is usually resolvable by discussion. It is a good idea, however, in audits which have been contentious or where there are significant disagreements to have a short discussion with the Director responsible just before the final report is issued. In this way the surprises can be avoided or at least minimised.

FUTURE FOCUS

The whole essence of the audit reporting process is to focus management attention on the issues which are important for their own function to move forward. I have seen reports where two pages of description are succeeded by comments such as 'the system is to be changed in the next eight weeks and the issues highlighted may therefore no longer apply'.

If there is no implication or benefit to the organisation in the future why raise it in the report at all? You cannot change what has gone.

MANAGEMENT COMMENTS

You need to ensure that the management comments received indicate commitment. 'Agreed' never gave me sufficient comfort that the action was really to be implemented. It is a good idea to push for a slightly more comprehensive response, particularly for the contentious issues. If management take the time to give considered responses, it is very likely that the actions will be introduced and will be done so on time.

AUDIT OPINIONS

It is regarded as good practice to incorporate a specific audit opinion in the report, under the heading 'Audit Opinion'. This is much better than expecting the reader to search for your opinion in the main body of the report or discover it as one of the conclusions.

There has been considerable debate about the merits or otherwise of giving an opinion by means of a scoring system such as 1 to 5 where 1 is awful and 5 excellent or a traffic light picture, red, amber and green. It is certainly true that the use of such scores on the face of the report is becoming less frequent.

The main reason for the abandoning the use of scores and replacing them with written opinions specific to the assignment is that a scoring approach, however well conceived, tends to lead to an argument with management. This is usually because they are not happy being graded as unsatisfactory when they believe that they are rather better than that.

The audit process is difficult enough without having conflicts regarding the often subjective grading being applied to their area, particularly if it means that senior management take a blame approach to dealing with the function.

I am very much in favour of the specific written audit opinion. Be careful, however, to avoid repeating the wording, however well meaning it may be, in various different reports. The wording is very important and should be focused directly towards the assignment and your overall evaluation of the effectiveness of the risk management controls and opportunities taken.

There is, however, one very good reason to create an overall measurable evaluation of the function being audited, using a scoring mechanism, as it allows you to answer the Audit Committee's most challenging question:

> Please give your overall annual assessment of the effectiveness of the risk management and control climate within the business and tell us whether this represents an improvement over last year.

This is an extremely challenging but totally valid question. An effective response can be given by accumulating evaluations of each audit carried out during the year and comparing this with the same evaluation last year.

Table 6.2 will illustrate a possible method:

Table 6.2   Overall audit opinion

	Excellent	Good	Effective	Poor	Very weak	
	9	7	5	3	1	
Audit area 1			✓			
Audit area 2		✓				
Audit area 3			✓			

Audit area 4			✓				
Audit area 5		✓					
Audit area 6		✓					
Audit area 7				✓			
Score		21	15	3			39
Maximum							63
Overall evaluation							62%
Scores							
More than 80% Strong							
60–80% Good							
55–60% Good apart from xxx							
40–55% Fair							
20–40% Poor							
Less than 20% Very weak							

The audit in question has seven specific areas which have been reviewed, for example, Cash and Bank, Debtors, Creditors, and so on. For each area an evaluation has been given using a score of 1 to 9. There will need to be accompanying criteria to ensure a consistent evaluation process, as per the following example.

Audit classifications

Audit classifications will use the following standard terminology:

Standard classification	Definition
EXCELLENT (9)	A very high standard applied throughout the function audited.
GOOD (7)	Although some opportunities for enhancement of control procedures were identified, the issues highlighted were not sufficiently critical to compromise the overall achievement of the control objectives reviewed.
EFFECTIVE (5)	Although the majority of control objectives were being met, the application of certain controls lacked consistency. Other controls compensated in part but timely corrective action is required by management.
POOR (3)	Certain key controls objectives were not being met. The issues identified, taken together or individually, significantly impair the overall system of internal control. Prompt corrective action is required by management to significantly improve the application of key controls.
VERY WEAK (1)	Lack of application of key control procedures was found to be so widespread as to undermine the system of internal control. This failure of the control infrastructure

has had, or is likely to have, significant implications for security, integrity or privacy. Urgent attention is required by management to implement effective controls.

Note that the headings have avoided the word 'satisfactory'; 'effective' is regarded as a much more positive and less non-committal word.

The score for each audit area is recorded and an overall score calculated. In this case the total score is 39 out of 63 or 62 per cent.

I am not advocating including the score in the report itself but simply using this evaluation to combine with all the other scores from the other audits to give an overall annual score. Adopting this approach will give you the information to answer the Audit Committee's question by saying 'Last year we have completed 84 audits, the average evaluation was 70 per cent. Last year the comparative score for the 79 audits completed was 63 per cent. Therefore there is evidence of an overall improvement.'

It could, of course, be argued that the audits were different this year to last making a direct comparison difficult but, assuming the number of audits completed is relatively large (50+), the comparison has validity as an overall evaluation of the control climate.

REPORTING ON THE MAJOR ISSUES

Hopefully the question about whether the observations and recommendations represent the key issues can be answered in the affirmative. You need to make sure that you are giving the correct emphasis in the report and focusing on the issues that really matter, rather than listing everything you did in chronological order.

An excellent approach and one which will significantly improve the likelihood of the less critical issues being implemented is to take the more minor issues off line. The way to do this is to cover each major issue in the report and then highlight the fact that there are another set of less critical issues, indicating the actual number of them in the report, which have been taken up separately and agreed with local management.

A separate schedule of these more minor issues, entitled 'Best Practice Ideas' or similar, should be prepared and issued to local management only. This approach has many benefits:

- The minor issues are not clogging the reports.
- Senior management are not generally interested in the low risk issues and will not need to read about them.
- Senior management will not react according to the number of issues raised. It is not uncommon for the Director responsible for an area to take a punitive stance towards the manager of the area being audited if there is more than say twenty issues raised. If only six key issues are raised they are much less likely to take this attitude.
- The report is more focused.
- With some of the pressure off, it is much more likely that the recommendations covering these issues will be implemented.

PRACTICAL RECOMMENDATIONS

Look back at the recommendations that have not been fully implemented and ask yourself the following questions:

- Was it because the recommendation was impractical to implement at the time?
- Was it too complex for the audit customer to bother with?
- Was this a very low priority issue for management and awkward to implement?
- Did it require a major systems change which could not be accommodated at the time?

Evaluating past recommendations in this way will provide a useful insight into the actions to take in the future. If the recommendation is known to be impractical for whatever reason, acknowledge the fact in the report; this may provide the necessary impetus for raising its profile.

For example, it is recommended that the dual entering of key data by the two departments, which is both inefficient and time consuming is rationalised. It is recognised that a major system change is required to accommodate this efficiency improvement and such a change can only be scheduled for Phase III of the project in 12 months time.

RISKS AND OPPORTUNITIES

The feedback on the audits will provide you with the answer to the question 'Was the audit recognised by management as being helpful by enhancing management of risks or identifying practical opportunities for the function?'

Specifically referring to the risks in the report is an excellent way of focusing management. Incorporating the risk matrix showing the inherent and residual risks together with your evaluation of the relative risks is an excellent approach.

Carefully wording the report to make the observations positive will also help significantly to focus attention on opportunities rather than problems. For example, instead of saying 'The following control weaknesses were found', it is much more positive to say 'A number of opportunities for improvement were identified'.

KNOWLEDGE AND EXPERIENCE

An excellent review tool for use by the audit manager assessing the audit is to reflect on the draft report (or, indeed, the final version) and consider the extent to which the report itself reflects the expertise and knowledge that was available.

Questions to ask are:

- Should more support have been available to inexperienced staff?
- Have certain areas only been superficially reviewed where more in-depth evaluation was necessary?
- If more than one auditor worked on the assignment, has the team worked together efficiently? For example, by allocating the work according to their specific skills?
- Should another auditor have been used on the assignment?

MANAGEMENT COMMENTS

Receiving positive comments, ideally in writing, is a real testament to the success of the audit process. Needless to say, the more you receive the better you are thought of. The testimonials you receive should be posted on your Intranet page.

It is possible to seek out positive comments. If it is clear that the audit customer is very pleased with the audit, you could ask if they would like to make a statement, which can be included on the Intranet. They can only say 'no' after all!

An excellent way of encouraging local management to implement the actions agreed is to garner a comment from the Director responsible for the function, particularly if the audit has been contentious and many actions are required. If you can gather a comment from the Director such as 'I believe that the issues raised are critical to the success of the function and the actions need to be implemented without delay', it will be very difficult for the local management to take no action. Obviously, such senior management comments will only be made on an exception basis, that is, only for certain key assignments.

COST BENEFITS ANALYSIS

Calculating the costs and benefits of the audit is an extremely useful way of focusing attention. Audits are expensive in terms of manpower, travel costs, and so on.

If you have not evaluated the cost of an audit before, it is well worth doing so. Take into account salaries, benefits, travel, administration, accommodation, and so on. In other words evaluate the total costs of the function and allocate this into person days.

As an example, assuming the total budget of your function is £1.2 million and you have 15 staff:

- average cost per employee is £80 000;
- average cost per day is £400*.

*This assumes that there are 200 audit days per annum after deducting holidays, training days, administration, and so on. The costs could be analysed further by seniority of employee if required but using an average will give a good guide.

An audit lasting 15 auditor days will therefore cost the organisation £6000. Calculating the cost of the audit and making the auditors aware of the true cost of an audit is an excellent way of ensuring that the team take the process seriously.

Assessing the specific benefits of an audit is much more difficult, of course, and was discussed earlier. If you can sit down to consider the benefits achieved, this is also an excellent way of assessing the achievements and reinforcing the positive aspects of the Internal Audit role.

The benefits do not have to be financial. Benefits could include:

- enhancing security;
- reducing the risk profile;
- improving protection against fraud;
- more responsive systems;
- better management information;
- best practice shared;

- reduction or removal of unnecessary controls;
- improvements in efficiency or staff usage;
- enhanced awareness.

Evaluating the benefits also provides an excellent basis for gathering the key information for the annual review to demonstrate the value added by Internal Audit during the year.

It is a very good idea to publish the benefits or opportunities in the report as this helps focus management attention. Unless financial benefits are totally provable, you need to be very careful about being specific.

A small but growing number of Internal Audit functions publish the cost of completing the audit, in monetary terms rather than person days of effort, on the face of the report, together with the benefits.

Those that have done so, report that highlighting the real costs has reinforced the message that the audit costs money, and if management do not take the observations and recommendations seriously they will have wasted time, effort and money. Such Internal Audit functions have reported a marked improvement in the implementation of the actions agreed.

AGREED ACTIONS

A simple change in the final report from using the word 'recommendations' to the phrase 'agreed actions' will also be a significant step in increasing the percentage of suggestions implemented. The draft report should include recommendations but in the final report incorporating agreed actions and the wording 'the new procedure will be implemented' rather than 'should be implemented' will have a major beneficial impact.

NAMED OWNERS

Having specific names alongside the actions agreed will further focus management attention. Many Internal Audit functions include the title of the person responsible instead of just his or her name. It is widely recognised that including the person's name will enforce the ownership and accountability for delivering the actions required.

The argument is that you can hold a person responsible but not a job title. Naming the action owner will also help ensure that, if the person changes roles before the action is scheduled for implementation, they (or their immediate manager) will ensure that the action is picked up by their successor.

FIRM IMPLEMENTATION DATES

Specific dates should be agreed and incorporated into the report. 'June 30th' is much better than 'Quarter 2'. The dates should be suggested by management rather than Internal Audit. The danger of Internal Audit determining the dates is that these may be reluctantly accepted by the audit customer but not really owned. If the date is missed and senior management follow up to determine why this is the case, local management have a ready excuse. 'Internal Audit forced the date on us and I never really believed it was achievable'.

Needless to say Internal Audit has the right to challenge the dates suggested by management. For example, if a simple action is given a date 12 months ahead for implementation, this should certainly be vigorously challenged.

A good technique to ensure that agreed dates are met is to encourage the executive in overall charge of the function to follow up local management two weeks or a month before the agreed date, depending on the elapsed time for implementation agreed in the report. Internal Audit should notify the senior manager of the follow-up dates as they occur to ensure that the control is applied.

EXECUTIVE SUMMARIES

All reports should have a short, ideally one page, Executive Summary highlighting the key points of the audit. The Executive Summary contents are discussed later in this chapter. The only exception would be if there is nothing or almost nothing to report, in which case one page will suffice for the whole report.

A very good practice adopted by many Internal Audit functions is to issue the Executive Summary in isolation to senior management. The real benefits are:

* Executives are very busy and will probably not want to read the whole report.
* They can ask for the main report on an exception basis. If they do, you know they are interested in the topic and it will then give you an opportunity perhaps to discuss directly the issues raised.
* They are less likely to overreact if there are many issues raised in the main report, as they will only hear of the very major ones in the Executive Summary.

If you currently issue the whole report to everyone, it is worth taking the time to ask senior management if they would prefer to receive the Executive Summary only.

Reports posted on the Intranet
The benefits were fully discussed in Chapter 7.

Action owners
There is nothing worse than agreeing actions with the personnel you regard as the process owners, only to find out after the report is issued, that they did not have the authority to do so.

Make sure at the clearance meeting that you check with the managers specifically that they do have the authority to commit to the actions. If not, you need to involve those personnel that do have the authority.

JARGON

Look at your reports, particularly the Executive Summaries, or get another function to do so, and identify any areas where jargon has been used. Ask whether the jargon was really necessary and whether you explained its meaning for the benefit of all.

One thing you can be sure of, if a senior recipient does not understand the jargon in the report, they will not come along and ask you what it means. You will simply be assessed as having failed.

ACTION PLANS

Having an action plan summarising the agreed steps to be taken, typically with the owners and agreed implementation dates, is one of the most significant steps to take to enhance the report and the implementation of the actions. The action plan, which is often the last page, can then be separated by management and used as the follow-up basis. It can also be used as the follow-up report by Internal Audit with the addition of a final column relating to status. An example action plan is included with the report template later in the chapter.

AUDIT COMMITTEE

The Audit Committee should be given the opportunity to receive either a copy of all the reports or for key audits. In either case, they should receive the Executive Summaries only. Either they can decide which are the key issues or you can if they so direct. The alternative is to produce a quarterly summary of the key points in the audits completed in that period.

CHIEF EXECUTIVE

The CEO (Chief Executive Officer) should receive a copy of all reports unless they specifically request not to receive those for the more routine, such as branch, audits.

MANAGEMENT ASSESSMENT OF REPORTS

If you are intending to make any changes to report formats or the reporting process, it is wise to ask senior management for their advice but also to ask them for their assessment of the reports as they stand.

A good method, which can also be used to assess the report yourself, is to ask for an assessment out of 10 for all or some of the following criteria, 1 being awful and 10 being excellent:

- objectives, how focused were they?
- scope
- clarity
- brevity
- balance
- reference to business objectives
- costs and benefits focus
- graphics
- future orientation
- management commitment
- risk orientation
- Executive Summary
- audit opinion
- praise where due
- practicality of recommendations
- jargon free
- action plans
- overall assessment.

CHANGING THE REPORT FORMATS

If you have not changed the report formats significantly during the last two years, it is highly likely that you should do so. Keeping the report interesting and fresh is the key to success.

IMAGINE YOU ARE THE RECIPIENT

If you had received the reports would they have spurred you into action?

This is an excellent self-assessment technique, to be used just before the report is issued. If you cannot answer the question in the affirmative, then it is highly unlikely management will either. You need to revisit the report and revise it accordingly.

BACKGROUND INFORMATION

In my opinion a large amount of unnecessary information is included in many Internal Audit reports. Sections on financial data relating to the operation can be easily accessed by the local management. It is their function, so what is the purpose of telling them what they already know? Long descriptions of what you did are also generally unnecessary: 'We examined 150 of these and 28 of those' is unlikely to be of any real interest to management. If they want to know, they can ask.

A few more examples are: 'We carried out the audit as part of the 2005 audit plan'. Of course you did, why else would you be carrying out an audit! 'We carried out the audit by a combination of interviews, testing and evaluation of key controls'. Is there any other way of completing an audit?

Make sure that you remove all the unnecessary information and the painfully obvious from the reports, concentrate on the issues that are important to management.

ARE YOUR REPORTS AS GOOD AS THEY COULD BE?

Even if you can answer the other 39 questions truly and honestly in the affirmative, I hope that anyone will agree that there is no such thing as a perfect audit report.

Professional standards

The Code of Ethics and International Standards for the Professional Practice of Internal Audit Performance Standard 2400 provides guidance for the content and focus of reports which correlates very closely with the expectations of Directors elucidated above.

Performance Standard 2420 – Quality of Communications, states that 'communications should be accurate, objective, clear, concise, constructive, complete and timely'.

The section entitled Criteria for Communicating (2410) provides, in my opinion, important guidance for the report writer. 2410 A2 Internal Auditors are encouraged to acknowledge satisfactory performance in engagement communications.

Again, I am a great believer in focusing on the positive in reports, as I will discuss in depth later in the chapter. The word I really dislike in this Standard, however, is the word 'satisfactory'. This is a word, which should, in my view, be avoided at all costs in an audit context. To explain why this word, which is used in almost every report I see, should be avoided, let me pose a question: If you sit down with your manager for your annual appraisal and they assess you overall as 'satisfactory', would you be pleased?

I would suggest that you would not be. The word satisfactory is one of a series of middle ground words, which are used when people do not want to commit themselves. It is akin to saying that something is 'nice'; it is very easy to misunderstand the sentiment.

Surely what senior management require from you is to give an overall judgement based on facts. You do not want to use words, therefore, which can be misinterpreted. You may mean satisfactory to be a positive comment but, if management receive it as a negative, you have problems. The words and phrases to avoid are discussed in depth later in the chapter.

THE PSYCHOLOGICAL DILEMMA

One of the biggest problems with the audit report itself and, indeed, the whole process of Internal Auditing, is that despite all your best efforts, the audit and its observations are invariably taken as a criticism of management.

The main reasons why the report can be seen as a criticism are:

- The focus tends to be on weaknesses and lack of control.
- The wording is often unfriendly and official, a common example seen in many reports is 'the procedures in manual 3B Subsection 6 Paragraph 4' or 'the regulations in the HSE Regulations 1995, section 57, subsection 2 paragraphs II and III are not being complied with'.
- The word 'audit' itself does not always have the most positive of connotations.
- Grudging praise. Very little real praise appears in most audit reports. Often the only attempt at praise is to thank the staff and management for their co-operation, which can often be seen by them as patronising.
- One of the biggest concerns is that the report will be seen by their boss and their boss's boss and there is a chance they will be subject to adverse criticism as a result.
- The reports are seen as distant or remote.
- It makes the manager feel as though they have failed.

Each of these concerns can be addressed:

- Weaknesses and lack of control. Focus on strengths, opportunities and the benefits to be achieved.
- Wording can be open and helpful, avoiding any implied criticism by sticking to the facts. Explain the reason for issues being highlighted, particularly the related risks. Under no circumstances quote specific regulations. The only reference that is needed is to the fact that there is a regulatory compliance issue and why it is important.
- Praise is a real key to unlocking success in report writing. Give the function recognition regarding the areas that are well managed or demonstrate that you understand the difficulties being faced, for example, significant absence of key personnel through illness, and so on.

If you highlight the good things first, it is much more likely that management will react positively to the opportunities highlighted. The way you refer to the opportunities will also play a significant role. An example statement, one which is often used, is, 'The following weaknesses in control need to be addressed'.

This could be worded as follows:

'The risks are being effectively managed but implementing ... would enable further competitive advantage to be gained'

or

'The well managed system could be made even better by ...'

- The issues about reporting hierarchy can be alleviated by taking the minor issues off line as explained earlier in the chapter.
- Reports do not need to be distant. Write them as though you understand their area of the business, as a partner rather than an external assessor.
- Supporting the management and the function will overcome the fear of failure.

How to link objectives, risk and audit observations

The risk-based approach, as previously explained, begins with the objectives, then examines the associated risks and then tests and evaluates the risks, the potential achievement of objectives and the controls in place to mitigate the risk. It therefore follows that the objectives, risks and controls should be linked in the report.

The functional management will understand the objectives, so, by referring to such objectives explicitly or implicitly will create an initial rapport. Referring to the risks and how well or otherwise the risks are being managed should then create an immediate recognition of the potential impact on the achievement of those objectives. Linking in the controls and the opportunities to enhance such processes should complete the picture.

An example might be:

The key objective is to ensure full data security. The main risks are deliberate or accidental access to unauthorised information. Twenty-three examples of security breaches were identified in July alone. The reason for the breaches (which were all benign) has been determined in conjunction with management.

Agreed Action

Access privileges will be amended with immediate effect to ensure access is on a need to know basis only.

The Executive Summary

The Executive Summary is the most important section of the report, without any doubt.

A good Executive Summary sets the tone for the whole report, and it:

- draws the reader in;
- highlights the most significant issues;

- promotes understanding;
- provides comfort that the issues will be addressed;
- gives specific assurance.

The Executive Summary is aimed primarily at senior management and should be written with this audience in mind. The wording should be clear, unambiguous and provide simple messages.

Imagine that you were met in the lift by your Chief Executive who is aware that you are currently finalising a report for a key audit assignment. If he asked you to tell him the key issues and he gave you as long as it would take for the lift to descend from the 10th floor to the ground floor, what would you say? You certainly would not talk about what you did; you would probably refer to three or four key points.

In practice you have rather longer than the thirty seconds allowed in the lift, but your Executive Summary needs to be just as focused.

The keys to successful Executive Summaries are:

- Draft the Executive Summary before the rest of the report. You will have gathered the key issues together following the clearance meeting with the management of the function being audited. If you can cover the four or five key points this will provide a good template for the more detailed part of the report.
- Keep the Summary to one page if you can.
- Start with a brief overview of the assignment (key objectives, and so on).
- Now focus on the key messages you want senior management to hear – hit them between the eyes.
- Be as positive as you can, unless the whole area is a shambles, in which case say so.
- Focus on solutions rather than problems.
- Summarise the actions that will be taken.
- Keep the language simple.
- Avoid jargon.
- Do not duplicate any of the wording in the main report.
- Quantify cost savings, and so on – but only if they are directly related to the audit.
- Show you understand the difficulties, for example if system changes are required.
- Focus on the issues in order of importance.
- Avoid descriptions of what you did.
- Do not try to score points at management's expense.

The best practice main report

- The main report is primarily aimed at operational management.
- Try and ensure that the issues are described simply.
- If you want action to be forthcoming, treat management with respect, they are the experts in their field, you are probably not.
- Do not use the report to belittle or criticise management.
- Be fair and objective.

The characteristics of the most successful reports, based on worldwide practice, are:

- Keep the main section of the report to three or four pages if you can.
- *Use the template in The Toolkit, Section 14 as your guide.*
- Keep appendices to an absolute minimum; ask yourself if management really need the detail. You can make it available to them if required without having to include it in the report.
- Arrange this section of the report in order of importance; you do not want the reader to have to reach page 5 before learning about the main issue.
- Use observations rather than findings.
- Keep the language simple.
- Avoid jargon.
- Unless the scope and objectives have changed during the assignment, in which case you need to refer to the changes and the rationale for the change, these should be as originally published.
- Cut down management comments if necessary; you do not need to cover them verbatim, but do feed back to management the actual wording you will be including (as a courtesy).
- Avoid long descriptions of what you did, numbers of documents examined, and so on; management either know already or are not really interested.
- Do not try to score points at management's expense.
- Get as many positive issues in as possible to ensure the report is balanced. This will greatly improve the likelihood that the areas for improvement are taken seriously.
- Avoid the word 'weaknesses'; use 'opportunities' instead.
- Focus on outcomes rather than output.
- Include graphics wherever possible.
- Use colour to enhance impact.
- Encourage positive management comments.
- Use agreed actions rather than recommendations.
- Put the circulation list at the back of the report; it is not the most important issue.
- The action plan should summarise the agreed tasks to address the opportunities raised in the audit.
- This should follow the same sequence as the report.
- The agreed actions should be précised and cross referenced to the report.
- The 'by whom' and 'by when' columns should be as detailed as possible.
- The status column is used in the follow-up process to record progress made; ideally it should be completed by management.
- The action plan can be used as the follow-up report.
- Be careful to ensure that you follow up any outstanding actions from the previous audit.

An example report follows:

KDGL INTERNATIONAL
INTERNAL AUDIT REPORT
Payroll
April 2005

Executive Summary

The audit was carried out to evaluate the effectiveness of the newly introduced payroll system, to ensure that appropriate controls were being applied.

The review was specifically requested by the Finance Director.

The payroll process was generally being operated effectively and it is pleasing to report that the system-based controls recommended by Internal Audit during our review during the development phase, have all been implemented.

Four significant issues were highlighted by this audit.

Two relate to personnel leaving the organisation – there is a risk that such leavers could continue to be paid after they have left.

A solution has been agreed with management and will be implemented without delay.

A significant problem with password security was also discovered, whereby unauthorised access to the whole system could be gained.

A solution has been agreed – personnel with the ability to access the whole system, set passwords, and so on, will be reduced to the absolute minimum.

The fourth issue relates to electronic payments.

There is a risk that the automated payment file once created could be amended – and fraud perpetrated.

This issue is to be investigated by the project board – two possible solutions have been offered by ourselves.

We are therefore very confident that this risk will soon be covered.

Objectives

The objective of this audit is to evaluate the effectiveness and efficiency of the payroll processes, with particular reference to the newly introduced IT system.

Scope

The boundary of this audit is the new payroll system. The secondary payroll maintained separately in Ireland is not included as part of the scope, this will be reviewed in June 2005.

Audit opinion

The payroll system is relatively new and as such is still in the process of being bedded in and developed. The controls within the system are effective in the main and the new team work very well together.

Conclusions

There are ten opportunities for improvement. Four we consider to be high risk and two medium risk. Work is in progress to resolve all the high-risk issues. As a developing system, management and the project team will need to ensure that controls are regularly evaluated and updated.

1. Observations

1.1   Difficulties were encountered with respect to staff leaving, as in 40 per cent of leavers reviewed the correct documentation was not submitted to HR and payroll. There is an ongoing risk that we will pay people their salary once they have left.

Agreed action point
New procedures have been implemented for leavers. Managers have been reminded of their responsibilities and also clear guidelines issued.

1.2   The legal department does not immediately chase up monies that are paid to staff who have left.

Agreed action point
Payroll has met with Legal and a new set of procedures implemented to recover monies paid to people who have left.

1.3   Too many people have system Administrator level passwords with the risk that access to the whole system can be gained by the 12 personnel involved.

Agreed action point
Payroll have agreed with IT to reduce the number of personnel with system administrator privileges from 12 to 2. Independent monitoring of access will also be instituted.

1.4   Once the automated payment file has been created the file is in text format and could easily be edited. There is potential risk that the integrity of the data could be compromised.

Agreed action point
The file format has been changed to enhance the control.

1.5   There is a difference in terminology between HR and Payroll concerning the definition of additional payments. Twenty-eight examples of pay differences were highlighted as a result.

Agreed action point
HR and payroll terminology has been synchronised. Further investigation found 124 errors, all of which have now been corrected.

1.6   Procedures need to be updated in line with new developments in the system so that if the designated member of staff is unavailable another member of the team can complete the necessary tasks.

Agreed action point
Payroll procedure notes will be updated in line with changes to the operation and functions of the payroll system.

1.7   Amendments are currently input twice, once by the business area and once by payroll. This is very inefficient and also very costly in terms of administration time.

Agreed action point
Single input of payroll amendments will be implemented in Phase 3 of the project in September 2005.

1.8   Sixteen examples of unauthorised overtime payments were found – such payments should not be processed without this authorisation.

Agreed action point
This was caused by the Payroll supervisor's absence and failure to notify the temporary supervisor of the required disciplines. Steps have been taken to ensure that this will not recur.

2.   Action plan

Ref	Agreed Actions	To be implemented by		Status
		Whom	When	
High Risk				
1.1	New procedures have been implemented for leavers. Managers have been reminded of their responsibilities and also clear guidelines issued.	James Steel	Implemented April 2005	Complete
1.2	A new set of procedures has been implemented to recover monies paid to people who have left.	Mark O'Connell	Implemented April 2005	Complete
1.3	The number of personnel with system administrator privileges will be reduced to two.	Bridget Davies	30 May 2005	In progress
1.4	The automated payment file format has been changed to enhance the control.	Bridget Davies	Implemented April 2005	Complete
Medium Risk				
1.5	HR and payroll terminology has been synchronised. Further investigation found 124 errors, all of which have now been corrected.	Mark O'Connell	Implemented April 2005	Complete
1.6	Payroll procedure notes will be updated in line with changes to the operation and functions of the payroll system	Sarah Ainsworth	30 May 2005	In Progress
Low Risk				
1.7	Single input of payroll amendments will be implemented in Phase 3 of the project in September 2005.	Bridget Davies	30 September 2005	Phase 3
1.8	Steps have been taken to ensure that overtime payments cannot be processed without authorisation.	James Steel	Implemented April 2005	Complete

Writing reports

WORDS AND PHRASES TO AVOID

Many of the common phrases as used in reports can be simply removed altogether without impact. They tend purely to be 'fillers'. The report will be much crisper and less wordy as a result.

Wording often used	Wording to use
1 It was found that ... For example, It was found that procedures for opening of new accounts were being compromised by lack of separation of duties, because personnel responsible for payments are also allowed to establish new accounts.	Exclude the phrase altogether, for example, New accounts are being opened by personnel responsible for payments thereby creating a fraud risk.
2 There is evidence of	Exclude the phrase altogether. (If there was no evidence you would not be raising the point.)
3 There is a problem with	Exclude the phrase altogether. (There must be a problem otherwise the issue would not be raised.)
4 It appears that ... or It seems that ...	Exclude the phrase altogether. (Avoid these 'unsure' words; the reader of the report would be entitled to ask why it only appears, have you not carried out enough work to be sure?)
5 There are weaknesses in ...	Exclude the phrase altogether. (Just explain the point you are making and avoid the phrase altogether.)
6 Some instance of ... were found or a few ... or many ... or a number of ... or most	Be specific as to the information provided. How many is some, a few or many? 3, 10, 20, 100? How many constitutes 'most'. It could be 51 per cent or 98 per cent. The best way is to refer to a percentage, for example, 26 per cent of the payments examined in ... were ...

7 There is conflicting opinion about ...	Specify the nature of the conflict and who the conflict is with, for example, You and management or management with another function.
8 We discovered that ...	Exclude the phrase altogether. (You have not discovered penicillin, have you?)
9 It was evident that ...	Exclude the phrase altogether. (I hope it was.)
10 Based on our examination or Based on tests completed	Exclude the phrase altogether. (What else could you be basing your observations on?)
11 Generally	Be more specific.
12 At the time of the audit ...	Exclude the phrase altogether. (Well, it is unlikely to be last year or next month!)
13 Our review showed that	Exclude the phrase altogether.
14 Satisfactory	Effective or Appropriate
15 Acceptable	Be more specific. (Acceptable to whom? How is this judged?)
16 Reasonable	Commit yourself. Reasonable assurance means to me 'I am going to avoid committing myself'.

Simplifying the report

- Keep the wording very simple.
- Keep sentences short and sharp (15 or so words is ideal).
- Ensure paragraphs have three or four sentences at the most.
- Use bullet points.
- Watch your pet phrases or words, particularly those that are fashionable; they quickly lose appeal.
  A few examples to be very careful with are 'proactive', 'results orientated', 'enterprise wide'.

As an example consider this observation:

There is a problem with the standard and consistency of the evaluations and reports on stock valuations carried out by the external agency. Differences in stock figures and regular write offs often without independent authorisation causes problems with stock availability. This requires additional visits by the agency to sort out the problems.

This observation has 50 words, but could be simplified quite easily without losing any of the key messages:

Regular stock differences and write offs, often without independent authorisation, have resulted in stock availability problems. Inconsistent disciplines operated by the external agency are a major contributing factor.

The revised observation has just 27 words.

More audit reporting ideas

- Do not include an explanation of the audit role in each report; put this on your Intranet site.
- Try to get a sponsor for each assignment. This executive will then be able to keep a watching brief over the outcomes and hopefully ensure that the actions agreed are taken seriously.
- Target the report to meet the needs of the management involved.
- Be on your customer's side; follow up actions with help, for example, to bring key personnel together to discuss outstanding issues.
- Keep sections and numbering of the report simple.
- Decide on one format and use it in all reports.
- Use an easily readable font size (12 point ideally) and a font that is different to your house style, if you are allowed to. Your reports will then stand out from the other documents received by management.
- Keep wide margins, typically 2.5 cm, as this makes the report much easier to read.

If you apply all or some of these best practice ideas, you will reduce your own risk and significantly enhance the reports and your reputation and added value.

7 Measuring Success and Marketing Risk-based Audit

What do management think of you?

One of the most important aspects of the Internal Audit role is often the least understood; this is the concept of adding value.

As a reminder, the Institute of Internal Auditors' definition states:

Internal Audit is an independent and objective assurance and consulting activity that is guided by the philosophy of adding value to improve the operation of the organisation.

But what is added value?
How do you measure it?
Can it be quantified?
Who should evaluate whether value is added?

A good start is to ask management what they think of the service provided and how they evaluate your function.

When my company (Business Risk Management Ltd) ask Chief Executives these questions in our periodic benchmarking surveys almost a third of them reply with this statement (or very similar):

The Internal Audit function provides a valuable service to the organisation but no specific measures are (to my knowledge) in place to evaluate their success.

This situation is quite extraordinary. I cannot believe that the same organisations do not attempt to evaluate the success of their marketing or procurement activities. Why then do they not evaluate their Internal Audit function? The most likely reason is that they do not know how to go about making such an evaluation; a number of respondents have said as much. How then do management judge Internal Audit in the absence of specific performance measures, in order for them to arrive at a view that the function provides a valuable service?

Have you asked your senior management formally or otherwise during the last 12 months for an evaluation? If not, this is a very sensible action to take and is certainly regarded as best practice.

The big question is how to ensure that you receive a valid and comprehensive evaluation. One very effective approach is to consult management before making any significant change in process and approach and then again six months later. You can then get an impartial 'before and after' assessment.

A number of issues will impact on management's evaluation of your success:

- The extent to which they have or will embrace the wide risk-based role for the function.
- The extent of challenges posed by them.
- How these challenges have been responded to by Internal Audit.

The reputation of your team and how to assess it

Internal Audit in every organisation has a reputation, good, bad or indifferent, and a key aspect of adopting a risk-based approach is to try to assess this reputation, and whether or not it is improving.

Risk, therefore, is not just something that affects the organisation; it directly affects the Internal Audit function itself. You might think that you are well thought of and local management might agree, but if senior management believe that better assurance can be provided via another approach, you might find that the function is suddenly outsourced; a situation encountered by a number of major Internal Audit functions, who thought highly of themselves.

How can you assess your reputation? The following methods are all tried and tested:

ONE-TO-ONE MEETINGS WITH SENIOR MANAGEMENT

Regular meetings with the ultimate decision maker for Internal Audit and other key influences are critical. The types of questions to ask are:

- What feedback are you getting from Board colleagues on the Internal Audit service? Is this mainly positive? What are the areas of concern raised?
- Has there been any specific feedback from the Chairman of the Audit Committee? What were the key messages?
- Have we focused our attention on the issues which you regard as the most important to the organisation's success?
- If there was one thing from your perspective that we could do to improve the service, what would that be?
- Have you any specific issues on which you would like us to focus audit attention, (for example, emerging risks or new business activities)?
- How well have we responded to challenges posed by the Board and the Audit Committee?
- We are planning to make the following changes in approach/audit report format/and so on. Do you think these changes will improve the service provided?
- What is the most important thing to you in relation to the Internal Audit service?
- Please give your assessment out of 10 for the quality of the Internal Audit activity and explain the reason for the score.

These questions could be asked in a questionnaire, but with senior management a one-to-one meeting is likely to be much more successful and informative.

POST AUDIT QUESTIONNAIRES

Many Internal Audit functions send out a questionnaire to the management of the function being audited immediately after the assignment has been finished. Unfortunately, whilst this is a very laudable activity, many functions report that the information received is not particularly useful.

Having seen many post audit questionnaires the main reason for this lack of impact, I believe, is that the questions that are asked and the scoring systems that are used do not lead local management into making an objective assessment.

Asking management to assess each aspect of the audit on a scale of 1 to 10 seems to be a good idea, but put yourself in the shoes of the manager who has just had a review of his area:

- Firstly, if the audit has highlighted many areas for improvement, the manager may not necessarily regard this as a benefit, particularly in a blame culture.
- Secondly, if you are asking whether the auditors were courteous and helpful, this may not be at all important to the manager. All that they can remember is the disruption caused.
- Finally, they know that you will be coming back in the future to carry out another audit and if they give you a low score, there is a chance you might give them a hard time next time.

A story might help to illustrate the difficulties:

I used to be a football referee (just at the amateur level) and each team was required to give their evaluation of the referee's performance in the match.

The scores given were often in direct proportion to which team had won the match. The winning team tended to give a score of seven to eight whilst the losers gave two to three. Clearly, as my performance could not possibly have been as inconsistent as the scores suggest, the value of such scoring was totally invalidated.

The same principle applies to post audit assessment. It is much better to try to assess performance in a simple manner, together with obtaining an opinion of the relative importance of each question. It is also extremely valuable to ask questions which cannot be answered by ticking a box or circling a score. An example would be 'How did you feel when you know an audit of your area was being planned?'

A sample audit effectiveness questionnaire can be found in The Risk-based Auditing Toolkit, Section 7 (see Appendix).

THE PERSONAL REPUTATION OF THE HEAD OF INTERNAL AUDIT

Are they regarded as a positive agent for change, seen as a member of the senior team, as a leader, as someone who is approachable and flexible – or not?

As in many functions, the person at the top sets the tone and the credibility for the whole activity; this is certainly true of Internal Audit.

THE EXTENT TO WHICH INTERNAL AUDIT ARE SEEN TO BE INVOLVED IN THE DEVELOPMENT OF THE ORGANISATION

Is Internal Audit involved in key business initiatives as advisor? Is Internal Audit involved in assessing new acquisitions or new activities? Does Internal Audit support other functions with advice and guidance? Is Internal Audit involved in the social life of the organisation (or do they stay away arguing it would interfere with their independence)?

THE EXTENT TO WHICH INTERNAL AUDIT IS INVITED TO ATTEND MANAGEMENT MEETINGS

Does management offer invitations to attend specific meetings where key developments are being discussed? Do you get an opportunity to inform about audits planned and the benefits for the audit customer?

THE EXTENT TO WHICH MANAGEMENT TRUST YOU TO ASK FOR ADVICE OR SUPPORT

Is Internal Audit asked for its opinions and advice? – not to cover the back of the requesting function, but as a genuine trusted resource.

Risk-based audit key performance indicators

The best way to demonstrate added value is to adopt specific performance measures (sometimes know as KPIs) and assess your performance against them. The following list (in no particular order) is recognised as the 20 best practice measures:

1   Feedback from Board and Audit Committee.
2   Elapsed time for issue of reports – completion of audit work to draft report
  •   This is totally under your control and best practice is two to three days.
3   Elapsed time for issue of reports – draft to final report.
  •   This is not totally under Internal Audit's control, of course, but the shorter the gap and the more pressure that can be exerted to get management comments, and so on, the better. Best practice here is seven to ten days.
4   Number of unsatisfactory audit opinions (as percentage of total).
  •   This indicates whether the business is improving by taking the audits seriously, and so on.
5   Number of audit assignments completed (versus number planned).
6   Percentage staff utilisation (direct versus indirect or audit and non-audit).
  •   Percentage of staff utilisation is how much direct time has been spent on audits (rather than administration, training, holidays, and so on). It is unlikely that it is practical to aim for more than 75 per cent utilisation.
7   Percentage of recommendations implemented.
8   Number of management requests.
  •   Number of management requests; the trend from year to year, the more requests you receive the more you are trusted.
9   Number of positive unsolicited comments about Internal Audit.

10 Number of complaints.
- Number of complaints appears to be a negative measure but the fact that someone has taken the time and trouble to complain at least shows they care enough about the audit activity to do so. The key is to ensure that you deal with such complaints quickly and effectively.

11 Number of repeat audit observations.
- Number of repeat audit observations; this may seem an unusual measure, but in practice the more repeat observations you make, the less impact you have had the first time, that is, you have not been persuasive enough to get management to implement the actions required the last time the audit was carried out.

12 Amount of measurable savings achieved as a direct result of audits.
- Amount of measurable savings achieved as a direct result of the audits; a great deal of discussion has been undertaken on the advisability of trying to measure savings as a result of audits. It is my firm belief that it is only worth using this measure if the savings have actually been achieved and were only achieved as a direct result of the audit. This KPI should therefore be assessed no sooner than 12 months or so after the audit.

13 Number of major process improvements implemented as a result of audits.

14 Percentage customer satisfaction (from surveys, and so on).

15 Percentage of key risks audited in the year.
- Percentage of key risks audited in the year: if you can demonstrate to management that you, for example, audited 40 per cent of the key risks (identified by them) in the year (and another 30 per cent in the previous year), you are able to make a much more positive and reliable statement about assurance to the Board or Audit Committee.

16 Extent of reliance External Audit can place on IA.

17 Audit coverage versus plan – geographic or business unit.

18 Cost versus budget.

19 Percentage of major systems developments reviewed.

20 Number of best practice ideas shared.
- Internal Audit can be accused of adopting a piecemeal approach. Opportunities are identified in individual reports for the benefit of the recipients of that particular report only.
- Publishing good ideas and opportunities highlighted (which could have similar positive implications for other branches, functions or activities) is an excellent way to demonstrate a value-added audit approach.

Probably the most important five are:

- elapsed time for issue of reports;
- percentage of recommendations implemented;
- percentage of key risks audited in the year;
- number of best practice ideas shared;
- number of audit assignments completed (versus planned).

Benchmarking

Whilst having performance measures in place, evaluating progress on a regular basis and reporting to the Board and the Audit Committee on such KPIs is an excellent approach, it may not be enough.

The Audit Committee, in particular, may well ask the following of the Head of Internal Audit:

> *We understand that you are well respected as a function and are performing well against the KPIs set but how do you compare with other Internal Audit functions in our sector or against worldwide best practice?*

This is not an unreasonable question, but how can you satisfy the Audit Committee in this regard? The best way is by benchmarking your function.

There are a number of options:

- The first is to use the Institute of Internal Auditors benchmarking service know as GAIN. This is a well regarded and comprehensive on-line questionnaire-based approach which provides a report covering many aspects of the Internal Audit activity and provides a comparison against overall and industry or sector trends.

  Full details can be found on the main Institute of Internal Auditors website (www.theiia.org).

- The second option is to prepare a questionnaire and send it to all the main organisations in your sector, collate the results and produce an overall report (without any details of individual businesses' data) where every organisation taking part gets a copy. The difficulties with this approach are:

  - There is a fair amount of work necessary to devise the appropriate questions, collate the results and produce and circulate the report.
  - Organisations in your own sector may be very wary of providing information which could be regarded (by some) as being sensitive.

  These difficulties can be alleviated by having an external organisation manage the whole process. My company has carried out a number of such reviews over the past five years both with very high response rates (typically 80 per cent of organisations respond to the questionnaires) and very positive feedback.

- The third option is to have an external organisation carry out a specific benchmarking exercise on your behalf, whereby all aspects of the Internal Audit service are benchmarked against worldwide best practice and a comprehensive report produced specifically for you. This is a service which has been provided by Business Risk Management Ltd for many different organisations across most sectors during the last five years.

A full explanation of this type of benchmarking exercise (which can also be used as a peer quality control review as required every five years by the Institute of Internal Auditors) can be found in the Risk-based Auditing Toolkit, Section 8 (see Appendix).

Marketing a risk-based approach

Our research indicates that one of the most significant differences between the Internal Audit functions that are recognised as highly successful and the rest, is that the successful ones market their service effectively.

At first sight it might appear unnecessary to market the function; surely management and staff know what Internal Audit is there to do and what they achieve. However, it is very likely that they do not!

One of the Internal Audit functions over which I had responsibility was already an established function when I was appointed to lead it. Everyone in the function told me that there was a clear understanding of the role at all levels within the organisation. I went out to speak to both senior and local management as part of my induction programme. Most people, it transpired, had very little idea of the role, some describing auditors as 'checkers' and many not even being able to distinguish between Internal and External Audit.

Anything that you can do to spread awareness and understanding of the Internal Audit role will pay dividends; this is particularly important if you have embarked or are about to embark on a risk-based approach. It will help you to:

- raise awareness;
- counter the negative stereotypes;
- highlight the value you can add;
- create demand for your services;
- develop better two-way dialogue.

You need to choose the marketing method and the messages well. They need to suit the culture and style of your organisation, but the following best practice ideas will give you plenty of choice.

INTRANET PAGES FOR INTERNAL AUDIT

All Internal Audit functions should have an Intranet presence. Your Intranet pages will provide an excellent marketing portal. The following information should be included:

- The Audit Charter – the terms of reference for the function, as approved by the Audit Committee.
- Frequently Asked Questions (FAQs).
  NB The charter is designed for more senior management. The FAQs should be written in a light, easy-to-read style, which is capable of being understood by any reader.

An example FAQ document is shown in The Risk-based Auditing Toolkit, Section 9 (see Appendix).

- A document called 'Common Misconceptions about Internal Audit' can be used in conjunction with the FAQs.

An example is shown in the Risk-based Auditing Toolkit, Section 10 (see Appendix).

- Audit plans for the next quarter or six months.
  I would not tend to put the whole 12 months plan on the site because it is likely that some of the audits in the second half of the year may need to be re-scheduled as priorities change. Some Internal Audit functions do not like the idea of giving the audit

customers advance knowledge about the forthcoming audit lest they 'put things right'. I would say this is a compelling reason for publishing the plans; you are not there to find management out, are you?

- Testimonials.
  If you receive positive comments in writing from customers on the audits or the service provided put them on the site (ask the customers' permission first, of course).
- Achievements.
  Do not be afraid to shout about your successes. Again these need to be attested and specifically achieved as a direct result of Internal Audit involvement. Many Internal Audit functions complain to me that major improvements and positive changes have been achieved as a direct result of audits but no one knows that it was Internal Audit that identified the opportunities. They won't if you don't tell them, will they?
- Performance against KPIs.
- Best practice ideas.
  The good practices identified via audits which may have wider application in the business.
- Profiles and photos of the audit team. Not all functions think this is a good idea but at least management and staff will know who you are and your experience, and so on.
- Internal Audit reports.
  This is certainly the most contentious inclusion on the Intranet site but it is something that a few functions are now doing. The reports need to be balanced and focused.
- Posting the reports on the Intranet site (with key working papers if you wish) is the natural extension to issuing the reports electronically and it is an excellent way to help change the culture to a much more open and sharing one.
- Annual report on the Internal Audit role, including the annual evaluation of assurance by the head of the function.
- Outlines of speeches or talks made at conferences by Internal Audit management.

DEVELOP AN INTERNAL AUDIT BROCHURE

Whilst this can be included on the Intranet site, it is often useful to have a professionally produced brochure to hand out, as not everyone will refer to the Intranet. The best brochures have an introduction by the Chief Executive which reinforces the message that the function is important and supported at the top level.

An example Chief Executive's introduction is included in the Risk-based Auditing Toolkit, Section 11 (see Appendix).

PRESENTATIONS AT MANAGEMENT MEETINGS

Being asked to attend management meetings is an excellent opportunity for marketing. Ask if you could do a short presentation (10–15 minutes only). Make sure that you make this customer focused; they will probably not be interested in how you carry out an audit, but they should be very interested in the benefits to them and how Internal Audit can help them achieve their objectives.

A PAGE ON THE MAIN WEBSITE

A short statement (excerpts from the Charter) highlighting the positive role of Internal Audit in Corporate Governance and the professional approach adopted. This provides confidence to website visitors interested in governance and control.

AUDIT NEWSLETTER

A simple newsletter issued periodically highlighting the customer focus and benefits of the modern approach to Internal Audit can be a very positive step. Avoid pages such as 'A day in the life of an Auditor'; these are usually not very credible to the reader.

ELECTRONIC SURVEY OF CUSTOMERS

Consider a six-monthly survey of customers (in addition to or as a replacement for the post-audit questionnaires). Publish the results widely, particularly focusing on actions to be taken by Internal Audit to address areas of concern which customers have highlighted.

OPEN HOUSE SESSIONS

Not for the faint-hearted this one – particularly if no one turns up. Set aside half a day and offer an open invitation for anyone to come along for ten minutes and learn more about what you do.

PUBLISHING BENCHMARKING RESULTS

If they are generally favourable.

INDUCTION PROGRAMME

Include a short section on Internal Audit in the Induction Programme for all new staff.

PROVIDING SUPPORT

Let customers know that you can help them get things done, that is, you can broker meetings between departments, for example.

GIVE CREDIT WHERE IT IS DUE

Make sure that you reflect the positive actions taken by management and the areas that are well controlled.

SECONDMENTS TO AND FROM INTERNAL AUDIT

The personnel involved will act as ambassadors for your function. Join in social activities such as quizzes or sporting activities within the organisation. Design your own logo.

The need to explain the process

The best way to ensure that there is a full understanding of the audit process and approach is to sit down with the management and key staff of the function being audited at the very start of the assignment, that is, the first day on site.

A short oral explanation can be given, in which case you need to prepare a short script to make sure that, whichever auditor delivers the words, the messages and content are the same. A better approach is to use a short five to ten minutes PowerPoint presentation, copies of which can be left with the functional personnel.

8 Corporate Assurance and the Internal Audit Role

The assurance challenges

More and more emphasis on governance, assurance and control is being espoused by recent regulation, standards and guidance, much of which is risk orientated.

How should the various assurance functions in a business rise to the challenge and how should the organisation manage such activities effectively and efficiently?

What role can Internal Audit take in ensuring a co-ordinated assurance statement is given to the Board and the Audit Committee?

There are now Corporate Governance requirements in place in most countries: beginning with the Treadway Commission in the US, the Cadbury and Hampel Reports and resultant Combined Code for Corporate Governance in the UK and similar developments in Europe, and most recently the Sarbanes-Oxley Act. Governance has grown in just a few years from being a concept to become the very pulse of the organisation and the way in which management of a company is judged.

So what does this all mean for the assurance providers? Who provides the assurance that the roles of the assurance providers are co-ordinated to ensure optimum comfort can be given to the Board and the Audit Committee?

The main assurance functions

The UK Combined Code for Corporate Governance in the UK recognises that there may be a number of different assurance providers:

In conducting its annual assessment, the Board should consider the scope and quality of the ongoing monitoring of risks and internal control, and, where applicable the work of its Internal Audit function and other providers of assurance.

COMPLIANCE

Compliance is a specific function, which has been enjoyed particularly by organisations in the financial services sector, primarily due to the requirements of the legislation in this sector. However, the increasing regulatory environment elsewhere, for example, in the utility and telecommunications industries, together with new EU directives, the Data Protection Act and employment legislation to name but three have significantly increased the pressure on businesses to comply.

As the penalties for non-compliance can be extremely punitive – including the ultimate sanction, the loss of the licence to trade – the risks are considerable.

The compliance function is therefore, of necessity, risk orientated but differs from Internal Audit in that, the compliance cannot be totally independent (as the function also has non-audit duties). This is not in any way intended to denigrate the compliance function – indeed in some organisations the heads of both departments report to the Audit Committee – but it does point to the need to co-ordinate the activities very carefully to avoid duplication and optimise added value.

Financial services organisations have developed excellent templates for such co-operation and these can provide a good skeleton to help businesses in other sectors tackle the subject of regulatory compliance.

HEALTH AND SAFETY

Many organisations have dedicated functions to monitor and review the effectiveness of the Health and Safety disciplines within the organisation.

Failure of employers to provide the following can again result in very significant fines and punitive action:

- safe systems at work;
- a safe place to work;
- plant and machinery that is safe to use;
- competent supervision and/or suitable training;
- care in the selection of employees.

Most organisations, however, tend not to evaluate health and safety in strictly risk terms, as one fatality, for example, is one too many. It is rare that Internal Audit, under whose umbrella responsibilities are passed down from the Board, review the effectiveness of the Health and Safety function or the risks associated with this topic. Encouraging these functions to work more closely together can only be beneficial to the organisation.

SECURITY

A different approach is increasingly being adopted, with security taking a much more proactive role. This is also tending to be risk focused, although in many businesses I have seen, the assurance risk focus has not permeated down to the security department. There is therefore a need for co-operation and education here – one which Internal Audit or risk management could promote.

RISK MANAGEMENT

Many organisations have recognised the advantage of establishing a dedicated risk management function, reporting through a Risk Management Committee to the Board. Many of these departments have evolved from an insurance base to become broad-based with wide responsibilities. Typically the risk management function is responsible for ensuring that a comprehensive risk management programme is developed and implemented and to ensure that the programme successfully enables the business to manage the many threats faced. In short it has responsibility for co-ordinating the risk management agenda.

It is therefore very important to ensure that all projects initiated within the business with a significant risk impact should be co-ordinated (if not owned by) this function, in order that risk is managed on a corporate basis (and the organisation is not suddenly caught in a downpour, or worse a flood).

Other assurance functions must develop a close liaison with risk management to ensure efforts are harmonised. This has been achieved in some organisations by a number of these providers now being managed directly by the risk management function.

ENVIRONMENTAL AUDIT

A number of organisations with particular environmental sensitivities, typically those in the chemical, nuclear and quarrying industries, together with those handling hazardous products, have established a separate environmental auditing function. These tend to audit against the environmental management system standard ISO 14000 and are of course risk focused. However, as well-publicised events in the nuclear industry have shown, the risks can be much greater than anticipated; in these cases fairly minor lapses have caused huge damage to the reputation of the businesses. Businesses in other sectors should therefore take heed. Environmental risks are likely to be significant for most organisations within the next few years (if they are not already). For organisations without an environmental audit capability, serious consideration should be given to buying in the expertise; this should help encourage the businesses to take the risks seriously, notably those posed by pollution and waste management.

QUALITY ASSURANCE

Many organisations have established quality audit teams to review all processes and activities covered by their quality systems, under the International Standard ISO 9000 (and its derivatives ISO 9001, 9002 and so on).

The role tends to be carried out by internal quality auditors who complete the audits on a part-time basis, either being employees of the organisation with other responsibilities or external personnel subcontracted to carry out the work.

These reviews are by necessity compliance orientated as the objective is to assess the extent of conformance with the quality procedures, but they are becoming more risk orientated as the functions and processes embraced by the total quality approach expands.

The standards for internal quality auditing are also becoming more stringent. It is now a requirement that internal quality auditors have sufficient recent experience and have formal auditing qualifications (all of which is incorporated in the Auditing Standard ISO 10011).

A real opportunity is therefore offered to refocus the activities of the quality audit team towards areas of significant risk, to assist in the Corporate Governance evaluation process. It also provides the opportunity for a much closer relationship between the Internal Audit function and the risk management team.

INSURANCE

Many risk management committees were originally established and led by the insurance manager – as a vehicle to build awareness of insurable risks and to help the organisation to introduce programmes and specific actions to reduce losses and claims. Whilst this was, and is, a laudable objective, most organisations have recognised that the majority of significant risks in a business are not insurable. To their credit it tends to be the insurance functions that have been leading the crusade to consider the wider risk agenda. Opinions vary as to the proportions of insurable to uninsurable risk, but a generally accepted model is that of the iceberg:

Just as only one tenth of an iceberg is visible above the sea so typically only one in ten of significant risks in a business are insurable.

It is therefore crucial that the insurance function is brought fully into the risk assurance process and that they have significant knowledge of the variety of risks impacting the business. In this way they can add substantially to the Corporate Governance process.

THE AUDIT COMMITTEE

The expectations and responsibilities of Audit Committees are becoming ever wider and, of course, now encompass risk. As recently as 2002 little mention of risk was made in many audit committee terms of reference. A survey of 155 companies carried out by KPMG at that time revealed the roles of the Audit Committee to be as follows:

	% of companies
Selection of external auditors	78
Assessing the system of internal control	74
Reviewing the scope and approach and results of external audit work	62
Accounting/reporting policies and procedures	51
Reviewing the results of Internal Audit work	31
Agreeing the Internal Audit plan	31
Agreeing audit fees	29

Since then the key focus has very definitely changed to include providing assurance that the company has effective processes for identifying and managing key business risks.

It is, therefore, the Audit Committee in many organisations that is taking the reins as far as the risk aspect of the assurance agenda is concerned – hence the logical and powerful role for Internal Audit in this regard. (IA is normally the only function with a direct reporting line into this body.)

It is, therefore, crucial for the Head of Internal Audit to build a very strong relationship with the Chairman of the Audit Committee, specifically to:

- recognise the audit committee as their client;
- understand the committee's expectation and respond accordingly;
- communicate with and meet regularly with the Chairman;

- communicate with the committee with candour and openness.

EXTERNAL (STATUTORY) AUDIT

External audit are also very much linked in with the whole Corporate Governance agenda given the reporting requirements that they have under the Combined Code, Sarbanes-Oxley Act, and so on. As a result, the external auditors are increasingly being asked to communicate qualitative judgements about accounting principles, disclosures and risk. By doing so, the external auditors can add to the effectiveness of the Board of Directors in monitoring corporate performance and risk management on behalf of the shareholders and in assuring that shareholders receive relevant and reliable financial information.

It follows therefore that a close relationship between the External and Internal Auditors (and to a lesser extent the other assurance functions) should exist.

It is my experience that in many organisations the external auditors have been unable to gain sufficient reliance from the Internal Audit function due to the fact that the Internal Audit programme was not focused at a high enough level. Focusing the Internal Audit activities towards the most significant risks provides an opportunity to enhance this reliance.

Internal Audit should therefore take every opportunity to develop a close working relationship with their external auditors, as much mutual benefit will accrue.

The opportunities for Internal Audit

Having worked in Internal Audit for 20 years and had close involvement with the other assurance providers, I have seen the roles change from verification and low-level checking to ones which in many organisations have carved out reputations for driving change and business improvement. The assurance providers, however, probably face the greatest challenge (and potential rewards) in their history.

This provides a potential 'shot in the arm' for the function, particularly as the provision does highlight the advantages of having an adequately resourced and professional IA function.

Nonetheless, outsourcing of in-house Internal Audit functions is happening in the UK, following a significant trend in the US. The Big Four firms of accountants and other specialists have, quite correctly, identified opportunities to provide high quality, competitively priced Internal Audit services on either an out-sourced or partnering basis.

I do not intend to discuss the arguments for and against outsourcing or partnering, but suffice it to say that the Big Four would not be providing the service unless they regarded it as a function that was important and would add value to their prospective clients. Exactly the same arguments apply to other assurance providers, particularly Quality Assurance, Environmental Audit and Insurance.

The challenges are those provided by the Combined Code in the UK, or the appropriate Corporate Governance requirements in other countries, and the business risk agenda in particular.

The converging role of the assurance providers

Whether in-house or externally provided, the focus of the assurance functions in the first decade of the twenty-first century has to be risk.

Audit Committees and Boards need the assurance functions to help them evaluate the effectiveness and efficiency of their systems of business risk management. This should ensure that the functions have a high profile, particularly if the business risk focus is communicated widely within the organisation (which it should be). For those functions, which have not specifically marketed themselves by means of a brochure, web pages, Intranet pages, newsletters and so on – this is an ideal opportunity to do so.

The high profile created and the necessity to give a considered opinion to the Board and the Audit Committee on the significant business risks and how effective they are being managed could also have negative connotations.

If the assurance providers have reported to the effect that the business risk management processes are effective and major problems or surprises subsequently occur, this could significantly impact on their credibility.

The key, I believe, is to co-ordinate the activities closely with the other assurance functions and, of course, management, to establish a clear agenda and the role and responsibilities of each function.

The need for multi-level reporting

Direct involvement of the Internal Audit and other assurance functions in the business risk and Corporate Governance arenas provides the opportunity to enhance the profile and recognition of the functions, but only if the reporting process is managed effectively. The assurance functions have the opportunity to report on a number of levels – each one requiring a different approach.

TO FUNCTIONAL MANAGEMENT

Reports to functional management on the perceived versus actual controls to mitigate key risks should focus on the opportunity to enhance control rather than a 'you said ... we found' approach. Specific benefits and business opportunities should be highlighted wherever possible. Actions must be agreed to tackle additional exposures before Board reporting.

TO THE BOARD

A quarterly summary of the results of the audits should be presented giving a picture of the overall accuracy of management's evaluations (in my experience, this having been generally sound) and an exception-based schedule of the impact on risk exposures – especially further or more significant exposures identified – together with the actions agreed to tackle them.

A quarterly progress report on the action plans to address the risk exposures identified in the business risk programme should also be presented.

TO THE AUDIT COMMITTEE

The Audit Committee report (at least three times a year) should focus on achievement:

- what actions have been implemented;
- the benefits achieved (monetarily if possible);
- the extent to which the risks have been reduced (using the risk matrix shown on page 100);
- what competitive opportunities have been identified/exploited;
- the percentage accuracy of perceived versus actual mitigation;
- the percentage coverage of the most significant risks achieved by Internal Audit.

How to co-ordinate the role with other assurance providers

Each assurance function within the organisation will have its normal reporting hierarchy – normally via the executive with responsibility for the activity. It is important to ensure that the messages received by the Board, the Audit Committee and Risk Management Committee are consistent and accurate. To do so requires co-ordination. This can be achieved in a number of ways: one way is for a nominated function (for example, risk management or Internal Audit) to receive reports from the other assurance functions on their activities and for the head of this function to extract the risk implications for onward reporting; another method is to have each function prepare a monthly or quarterly report, specifically relating to risks covered and the key findings. These reports can then be put together into a pack (with a summary) for onward transmission to the Board and so on. This method has the advantage of enhancing ownership; a third approach is to circulate individual reports widely between the assurance functions and ask the heads of the departments to compare and contrast the findings with their own – enabling reports for their executives to be more balanced.

I favour a fully co-ordinated approach with one function taking responsibility for extracting the key issues (with accompanying reports from each assurance function). A simple method of ensuring that there is no duplication of effort or too many assurance functions visiting the same function at the same time, to tackle what management often regard as a similar review, is to meet regularly with the heads of the other assurance functions.

A quarterly meeting can achieve much:

- share plans for the next quarter and agree not to visit the same functions or locations during the same period;
- identify areas of possible overlap and agree an approach where only one function covers each area – using a risk-based evaluation;
- share the key observations from the audits and reviews and discuss common issues;
- once a year prepare a consolidated report for the Board with a section for each assurance activity. In this way a comprehensive assurance position statement can be developed.

CONCLUSIONS

The governance and business risk challenges provide considerable opportunities for the assurance functions in a business to demonstrate their important contributions. A much more co-ordinated approach is, however, necessary if this is to be truly successful.

The following is a suggested model or paradigm:

Table 8.1   How to optimise assurance

Current approach	Required approach
Assurance functions' roles and responsibilities less than clearly defined.	Very clear terms of reference for each function defined and approved by the Audit Committee – to ensure no overlap (misunderstanding).
Assurance functions have separate reporting lines and are not co-ordinated.	Reassess reporting lines – ensuring all report to a Board Director. Establish a clear written method of co-ordination – responsibility being given to one of the assurance functions. Heads of functions should meet together quarterly. Share annual plans. Agree not to visit same location in the same quarter. Determine optimum function to review each area.
Assurance functions have different objectives and not all formally consider the implications of risk.	Ensure objectives of each function embrace risk and clearly identify the roles and responsibilities in relation to risk reporting.
Internal Audit may not base its programme on the most significant risks in the business.	Internal Audit should ensure that at least 60 per cent of its programme is directly based on the most significant risks identified by management. (Best practice statistics from the Business Risk Management database).
Role of Internal Audit and other assurance functions in the business risk process often poorly defined.	Audit Committee and Board to agree specific role of Internal Audit and other assurance functions in the development of the business risk programme.
Assurance functions are afraid of getting too involved in CSA or risk workshops lest their independence be compromised.	Get as involved as possible (as this will add the greatest value). Define the boundaries carefully and recognise that the role is not 'audit'. Independence will therefore be unaffected.
Mix of skills in many assurance functions is limited.	Develop skills and competencies using the competency framework as the basis.
Many assurance functions are not properly represented on the 'top table'. As a result their contribution is not valued as it should be.	The business risk and governance agenda provides a significant opportunity. All functions must therefore demonstrate what they can do – and therefore earn the recognition they deserve.

Assurance functions are often accused of not working together with management.	Co-ordinating activities and leading CRSA activities will build much closer relationships and enhance trust.
Many reports produced by assurance functions are lack-lustre and fail to promote change.	Refocusing reports on risk and making them much more positive will transform the value delivered by the functions. At least once a year provide a joint report to the Audit Committee or Board – with input from all assurance functions.

Ever-increasing shareholder expectations and the need to achieve demanding growth, profit, safety, environmental and other regulatory targets push organisations into taking bigger and greater risks. As a result senior management need much greater levels of assurance that the risks are being managed effectively across the organisation. To provide this comfort, an effective risk management and control framework is essential. As a result independent, positive assurance that such frameworks are effective and efficient is vital. Professionally focused and co-ordinated assurance activities will ensure the best possible service to senior management.

If Internal Audit can take up the challenge to bring together the various assurance providers and can achieve the goal of providing fully co-ordinated Board assurance they will certainly be well rewarded in terms of recognition and reputation.

9 *The Future*

The next horizon – assurance-based audit?

Risk-based auditing, as hopefully I have demonstrated, provides the opportunity to:

- audit the things that really matter;
- enhance the reputation of Internal Audit;
- provide measurable added value;
- refocus your reports to enhance their impact;
- create a partnership with management;
- break down the barriers;
- work with management to help them manage risks;
- identify greater opportunities for the organisation;
- focus on the future rather than the past.

Whilst all this is true, the interesting question is 'Where will Internal Audit be in ten years time; how will the function develop further?' I believe that the answer lies in the even greater development of Corporate Governance. It is likely that more and more pressure will be exerted upon Boards of Directors and Audit Committees to be even more transparent about how effectively the business is being managed. There is a noticeable trend for more and more external regulatory assessments across all sectors and countries and I firmly expect this to intensify at least until the end of the decade.

So what does this mean for Internal Audit?

The likely answer is the development of assurance-based audit. Corporate assurance is a title that has already been adopted by some Internal Audit functions, thereby removing the negative connotations potentially associated with the word 'audit'.

I am not sure whether the abandonment of the Internal Audit title is a positive step, as Internal Audit is a profession with its associated standards but, if the change of title assists the function to shake off the negative image for certain organisations, it is easy to see the attraction.

The definitions of corporate assurance being used by functions that have adopted this wider brief demonstrate the evolution of the role. An example is:

To provide an independent and objective opinion on the adequacy and effectiveness of the processes in place for Risk Management, Control and Governance.

Certain Internal Audit functions adopting this wider brief have taken over direct responsibility for Health & Safety, Insurance, Security and Risk Management in addition to the audit role. In this way, they can provide an overall evaluation and assurance of the whole organisation.

This may be a step too far for many Internal Audit functions and it can clearly be argued that there is a danger of taking on line responsibility which may compromise independence. It is certainly true, however, that the ability to give a co-ordinated assurance statement to the Board and the Audit Committee is enhanced as a result.

The role of the Audit Committee is now being extended to include responsibility for ensuring that arrangements are in place to provide the necessary level of assurance to meet the organisation's current and future needs. This has led to the appointment in some organisations of a 'Head of Corporate Assurance'. The role includes the requirement to make an assessment of the extent to which the total assurance requirements of the organisation are met and will continue to do so in the next two to three years.

It is not necessary to take responsibility for all the assurance activities in the organisation to be able to provide co-ordinated assurance evaluations but the need to bring together the often disparate assurance reports and opinions provided in many organisations will become more and more critical.

The future of Internal Audit – feast or famine?

Those functions which adapt to the challenges of risk and assurance will thrive and prosper. Those that continue to provide an inward looking, traditional compliance-based approach are unlikely to survive. Many such functions have already been outsourced to external organisations.

Be warned! Your Internal Audit function needs to change as rapidly as your organisation or it will die.

Globalisation and the implications for Internal Audit

The world is changing so rapidly, with the national and international barriers increasingly being removed that Internal Audit is flourishing in all corners of the globe.

Did you know that more students in China now take the Institute of Internal Auditors' professional examinations than the rest of the world put together?

There has never been a more exciting time to be an Internal Auditor, nor more chance of developing an excellent career for yourself, both within and outside the function than in the second half of the current decade.

Environmental Auditing is developing as a hugely important brand of auditing, as is Corporate Social Responsibility Auditing. The development of advanced skill training for Assurance Providers demonstrates the exciting possibilities.

Whichever country you live and work in, the opportunities to influence your organisation in a positive manner and add measurable value have never been greater. All you need to do is grab the chance with both hands.

Conclusion

For those readers about to embark on the risk-based auditing journey, I hope that I have provided you with enough idea for mapping out your route.

For those of you who have already implemented a risk-based approach, I hope that you have been able to gather some further inspiration to enable your function to achieve even greater success.

Let me leave you with the definition of a miracle:

Doing exactly the same tomorrow as you have done today and achieving completely different results.

And you don't want to wait for a miracle, do you?

The Risk-based Auditing Toolkit

Section 1: Introduction

The toolkit is designed to provide Internal Auditors with tools, techniques and information to enable a risk-based approach to be adopted. The toolkit is arranged into 14 sections.

- Sections 2, 3 and 4 relate to supporting the development of a formal process for evaluating and managing risk.
- Sections 5 and 6 relate to skills and audit methodology.
- Sections 7 and 8 relate to evaluating the effectiveness of the internal audit service.
- Sections 9 to 11 provide ideas to market a risk-based approach.
- Sections 12 and 13 relate to planning the audit.
- Section 14 provides a best practice audit report template.

Section 2: Memo to launch the business risk programme

To	See Distribution	Date		From	CEO
cc		Ref		Ext.	

BUSINESS RISK PROGRAMME

Introduction

As the business environment becomes ever more complex and the competitive pressures even greater, it is crucial that we fully understand the threats and opportunities impacting the company.

Consequently, I have decided to instigate a formal programme to evaluate these risks and opportunities.

The programme will be based around facilitated workshops. The first workshop will be with the Board at which the key risks and opportunities will be identified and evaluated. Following this, a further workshop will be held with functional heads and Divisional Executives, to assess mitigation for each key risk and identify any exposures or unrealised opportunities.

Phil Griffiths of Business Risk Management Ltd, an organisation with specific expertise in this regard, will facilitate the programme. He will be supported by John Smith, Head of Internal Audit.

Workshop 1 Objectives

The 'deliverables' from this workshop will be:

- identification and recording of the key risks and opportunities;
- evaluation of the risks based on likelihood of occurrence and monetary impact;
- weighting of the risks and opportunities by means of a risk matrix.

This workshop has been designed to take a broad and strategic view of all the vulnerabilities in the business, as opposed to merely financial or operational risks.

Workshop 2 Objectives

The 'deliverables' form this workshop will be:

- recording of mitigation for each key risk;
- evaluation of the effectiveness of such mitigation procedures and identification of any exposures;
- assessment of exposures and recording of actions proposed;
- matching of risks to objectives;
- development of action plans and assigning of responsibilities.

The output will then be consolidated and widely communicated.

It is anticipated that the programme will also help us to:

- better achieve our strategic objectives;
- improve the quality of our business decisions;
- manage our resources more effectively;
- satisfy regulatory requirements;
- anticipate and respond to changing social, environmental and other requirements in a proactive and systematic way;
- provide greater protection for our investment;
- reduce the cost of risk;
- reduce the number of surprises;
- minimise the cost of insurance;
- provide the opportunity to focus the Internal Audit programme specifically on the most significant areas of risk.

<u>Pre-Workshop Preparation</u>

You are requested to read and think through the list of 'Diagnostic Questions' attached and relate them to the context of your business or discipline. As a result, try to identify the experiences or events within the business that suggest specific areas of risk and vulnerability? What are the new risks and vulnerabilities that could emerge in future? It is suggested you note down risks or threats as they occur to you and bring them with you on the day.

You may also wish to reflect on the following 'food for thought' questions:

- What are the major drivers of change (political, economic, social cultural, technological) in our business environment? What are the implications for the business?
- What are the 'unpleasant surprises' if any that you've had in this business in the past? How have you recovered from them?
- Do you recall any major lost opportunities for your business? How could they have been avoided? What are the factors that could lead to similar opportunities being lost in the future?
- What are the two or three most concerning facets of this business? Imagine that a competitor was endowed with unlimited power to destroy your business. What would be the simplest and quickest way to do so?
- Have there been any significant failures by competitors? What is your understanding of the factors that brought these about?

Diagnostic questions

- What are the key market needs the business serves? Is demand robust?
- What are the tangible and intangible resources and assets deployed in the business? Are they secure?
- What drives costs in the business? Is the cost structure stable relative to competitors?
- What is the profile of the customer base? Is it stable? Is there an over-dependence on one or a few customers?

- Is there a fundamental technology that is incorporated in the product or in the process used to make it? What may make it obsolete?
- Does our business have any 'special abilities', that is, certain things that we do extraordinarily well or far better than our competitors? What underpins these?
- Are there any strong corporate identity symbols (for example, brands, corporate name, distinctive packaging, and so on) that are important in the business? Would the loss of these be damaging?
- Is the business dependent on any barriers (tariffs, patents, licensing requirements, and so on) that fence competitors out? What would happen if these barriers were removed?
- Is our market affected positively or negatively by any specific social or cultural values (for example, ecological concerns, attitudes towards foreign investors, and so on)?
- Are there any government or other sanctions under which we operate (licences, accreditation)? Are there other supports and incentives (for example, tax concessions on mortgage interest)? Are there any indirect subsidies on which we are reliant?
- Under what conditions might we experience a significant loss of customer trust in the integrity of our products and organisation? What liabilities and damages might result?
- Is the market for our business related to the availability and quality of complementary products or services, which we do not influence? If so which?
- Are competitors able to steal an advantage over us in securing lucrative business from current and potential customers?

Section 3: Outline agenda for business risk identification workshop

MINIMAL PERSONAL INTRODUCTIONS – 5 MINUTES

For the benefit of relative outsiders, for example, external auditors. Check that everybody knows everybody else, and move on.

OBJECTIVES/GOALS FOR THE DAY – 5 MINUTES

Deliverables are:

- record of key risks and opportunities;
- completed risk matrix;
- schedule of prioritised risks.

GROUND RULES – 5 MINUTES

- boundaries of discussion are none;
- no hierarchies – park egos outside the door;
- no hidden agenda;
- opportunity to say what you feel;
- suspend judgement until asked to apply it;
- build on agreement, revisit areas of disagreement later;
- everybody to contribute;
- listening skills;
- time management – 'come what may', guillotine will apply.

BACKGROUND AND CONTEXT – 30 MINUTES

Background/context of workshops, focus on benefits to business and emphasise that the first workshop aims at analysis only as opposed to reviewing/debating risk mitigation procedures.

- imagine these newspaper headlines;
- definitions;
- wrong assumptions about risk;
- sector developments;
- risk cultures;
- surprises;
- why business risk is such a hot topic;
- benefits of a formalised approach to risk management;
- how to measure risk;
- inherent and residual risk;
- categories of risk;
- the need to integrate risk with business planning;
- using a risk matrix to prioritise actions.

RISK IDENTIFICATION – 20 MINUTES

Determination of risks – monetary minimum to be set:

- Participants invited to think of as many as possible, and short term as well as long term possibilities. No idea to be excluded, however improbable it may appear at this stage. Inherent risks not residual.
- All participants will be supplied with Post-it® pads, and asked to write each idea, telegraphically, on a sticker. The facilitator should throw in ideas and prompt where necessary.

RISK CATEGORIES – 5 MINUTES

The seven risk categories will be offered as an approach.

BREAK – 10 MINUTES

EXERCISE 2 – 'SIFT' – 40 MINUTES

Participants will be invited to stick the Post-it® notes on the most relevant flip chart on the wall – representing the seven categories. The participants will now be encouraged to view the output and complete further stickers if they can identify any additional risks.

Now allocate two or more persons to each category and ask them to sift and cluster the output.

- Add, based on risks not adequately covered.
- Eliminate – where there is a direct duplicate
- Cluster, where two or more stickers make reference to the same risk.
- Clarify, where the meaning of any sticker is not clear.
- Negotiate with other 'owners' where the risk is felt to be on the wrong chart.

FEEDBACK – 20 MINUTES

Each team now reports back to the full group to ensure that everybody appreciates the full range of risks identified. Risks on more than one chart can now be combined.

INPUT – PROBABILITY AND IMPACT ASSESSMENT – 5 MINUTES

Some simple ideas will be offered to ensure that everyone uses a similar scoring scale.

RISK MATRIX – 60 MINUTES

Each risk cluster will now be scored as per the matrix. This will usually generate a good deal of discussion. Two or more syndicates may need to be formed for this part of the workshop if the number of participants is more than 12.

After reflection, a group view on impact and probability of occurrence will be elicited, and will be plotted on 'Matrix'. Code numbers may be used for plotting.

NEXT STEPS – 15 MINUTES

Output process – review and next workshop will be covered.

TOTAL TIME 3.5 HOURS

Section 4: Risk register

1	2	3	4	5	6	7
Area of risk	Inherent risk 1–9	Mitigation/ controls in place	Residual risk 1–9	Actions recommended	By whom By when	Risk owner

Section 5: Auditors' skills evaluation

Skill	Auditor 1	Auditor 2	Auditor 3	Auditor 4	Manager 1	Manager 2	Action planned
Communication							
Written	6	4	8	5	8	7	Report writing course auditors 1, 2 and 4
Verbal	8	7	7	5	6	8	
Auditory	7	5	7	8	8	8	
Facilitation	n/a	n/a	6	6	5	6	Facilitation skills training
Business knowledge							
Banking	4	8	6	3	9	8	Auditors 2 and 3 on banking audits – train others NB auditors 1 and 4 taking banking exams
Insurance	6	3	8	7	7	5	
IT	3	8	4	3	3	9	
Pensions	4	2	8	6	8	3	
Results driven	6	7	7	8	8	8	
Negotiation	3	4	5	4	6	5	Whole team on negotiation course
Open mindedness	6	3	6	7	7	8	

Section 6: Audit methodology

Strategic planning

Develop audit universe

Determine the level of assurance required

Prioritise audits by means of the risk model

Prepare audit priority schedule (three-year plan)

Separate into annual plans

Develop quarterly plan

Publish quarterly plan

↓

Assignment planning

Develop draft objectives

Determine business objectives and risks

Set up pre-meeting

Hold pre-meeting with management (one month prior to the audit)

Agree audit objectives and scope

Develop audit programme

Determine personnel to interview

↓

Completing the assignment

Prepare audit file

Give pre-audit PowerPoint™ presentation

Interview key personnel

Record the process (or update previous records)

Carry out walk-through tests

Determine level of further testing required

Complete testing

Record evidence and prepare discussion points

Hold clearance meeting

Complete audit checklist

Complete personal learning planner

Audit reporting

Prepare the draft report

Discuss with manager (if appropriate)

Audit management review (where appropriate)

Issue draft report

Discuss draft with management

Incorporate management comments and make necessary changes

Issue final report

Follow up via action plan

Summarise key issues for the Board

Section 7: Audit effectiveness assessment

It is very important to get feedback from the audit customers as to the value added by the audit. This can be achieved in a number of ways. Always consult your manager first – as they may want to carry out this research themselves.

The first is face to face – ask the key contact what they thought about the audit; the second is by phone; and the third is to issue a questionnaire – this is normally the least effective – but it may be appropriate for senior management – say on a quarterly basis.

The following table in the questionnaire is intended to provide you with guidance on the issues to raise – you will probably want to select a variety from the table.

Audit Effectiveness Questionnaire

The 'Audit Effectiveness Questionnaire' is designed to evaluate your experience with the audit and how you feel we performed. You are requested to rate the actual performance level relative to your expectations by circling an appropriate number (4 is highest performance level) and then indicate the importance of the criteria to you.

Criteria	Performance rating	Importance of criteria to you
You were notified of the planned audit on a timely basis.	1 2 3 4	1 2 3 4
The scope/objectives of the audit were made clear to you before the audit commenced and you had the opportunity to give your views.	1 2 3 4	1 2 3 4
The areas covered during the audit were of significant importance to your business activities.	1 2 3 4	1 2 3 4
Your suggestions and considerations with respect to what the key areas are and which should be covered by the audit were taken into account.	1 2 3 4	1 2 3 4
You were kept up to date on audit observations and potential recommendations during the audit process. The closure meeting contained no major surprises.	1 2 3 4	1 2 3 4

Criteria	Performance rating	Importance of criteria to you
We minimised the disruptions to your business as much as possible.	1 2 3 4	1 2 3 4
The time we spent on site at your location was reasonable.	1 2 3 4	1 2 3 4
Audit recommendations proposed during the audit: ❑ will contribute to the achievement of your objectives ❑ were practical ❑ are cost effective ❑ will add value to the business	 1 2 3 4 1 2 3 4 1 2 3 4 1 2 3 4	 1 2 3 4 1 2 3 4 1 2 3 4 1 2 3 4
The final report was: ❑ accurate ❑ brief ❑ balanced ❑ a fair reflection of the situation at the time of the audit ❑ jargon free ❑ free from nit picking ❑ issued a short time after the final fieldwork was completed.	1 2 3 4 1 2 3 4 1 2 3 4 1 2 3 4 1 2 3 4 1 2 3 4 1 2 3 4	1 2 3 4 1 2 3 4 1 2 3 4 1 2 3 4 1 2 3 4 1 2 3 4 1 2 3 4

How did you feel when you heard that an Internal Audit of your area of responsibility was being planned?

With respect to your recent experience please list up to six words, which you believe are appropriate to describe internal auditors or the audit process.

Give an example of something you think Internal Audit has done well and you would like to see more of.

Give an example of something you think Internal Audit could do differently or you would like to see less of (or what is the one thing that we could do next time to make things better for you).

Thank you very much for taking the time to respond to these questions.

Section 8: Proposal for Internal Audit department benchmarking review

1 EXECUTIVE SUMMARY

The following proposal outlines the suggested approach and methodology for conducting an independent benchmarking review. All aspects of the audit process will be evaluated against worldwide best practice. The Business Risk Management Global Internal Audit database (currently with information from over 3300 Internal Audit functions) will be used as the basis.

Over 200 aspects of the Internal Audit activity, its documentation, relationships, outputs and success measures will be reviewed and evaluated against the BRM unique benchmarking scorecard.

The audit process is evaluated under 11 sections – as detailed in Section 2. Each section is evaluated in turn by means of interviews with key personnel and review of all documentation and a score given – with opportunities for improvement identified where necessary.

A comprehensive report will be prepared for discussion with the Head of Internal Audit. The report will incorporate an overall benchmarking score – including the relative overall position occupies compared to other functions in the BRM database. A detailed evaluation of each of the 11 sections will be included in the report. For each section reviewed the strengths, opportunities and recommendations will be highlighted.

An Executive Summary Report will also be prepared summarising the scope, approach, observations, recommendations and actions agreed.

The consultant in this assignment will be Phil Griffiths, Managing Director of Business Risk Management Ltd, A Chartered Accountant with over 25 years experience in the field of internal audit and risk management as practitioner, professional adviser, facilitator and trainer. He has carried out regular benchmarking exercises on behalf of clients in both the UK and abroad.

2 SCOPE, APPROACH AND METHODOLOGY

The scope covers all aspects of the Internal Audit service and is separated into 11 sections for the purpose of the review:

- the Audit Charter
- professional standards
- the Audit Committee and the IA role
- Corporate Governance and the IA role
- skills, training and resources
- strategic audit planning
- managing the audit assignments
- measuring performance
- marketing the IA function
- the audit files, procedures and records
- the Audit Report.

Each activity will be assessed by reviewing all documentation, files, and so on, and by interviews with key personnel.

Phase 1   Review of documentation
The Audit Charter
- assessment against best practice
- endorsement by Audit Committee
- communication
- the reporting line of the function
- incorporation of IIA standards
- scope of the function
- the role and how it is evolving.

Professional standards
- formal adoption by the Audit Committee
- monitoring of compliance
- evaluation of integrity, objectivity, confidentiality and competence
- the balance between compliance, assurance and consulting
- due professional care
- internal QA process
- resource management.

The Audit Committee and the Internal Audit role
- overall relationship
- attitudes towards IA
- evaluating the Audit Committee requirements
- requests
- issues reviewed with the Audit Committee
- Audit Committee reports
- feedback on performance
- challenges
- annual assurance statement by IA.

Corporate Governance and the Internal Audit role
- the role in the Corporate Governance process
- role in risk management
- the risk focus of the function (and the relative roles of other assurance providers)
- co-ordination with the other assurance providers
- the External Audit relationship
- expectations of the Board, executive management and operational managers
- Board feedback
- meetings with Chief Executive and other Directors
- Sarbanes-Oxley implications
- role in fraud prevention and investigation
- combined code compliance.

Skills, training and resources

- audit personnel – numbers, skills, experience and so on
- job descriptions
- measures against database, for example, number of auditors versus number of employees
- training plan
- performance
- breadth of expertise
- resources and coverage
- functional costs
- movements of people
- relative experience.

Strategic audit planning

- approach adopted
- determining the level of assurance required
- the audit universe
- partnering
- the sources of audit work
- management requests
- geographic and business unit coverage
- coverage of specialist areas (treasury, IT security, and so on)
- scope and frequency of assignments
- non-audit work
- the future direction of the function
- the challenges faced.

Managing the audit assignments

- fieldwork techniques
- tactical audit planning
- audit programme development
- risk assessment
- audit assignment planning and control
- the use of technology – audit automation, computer-assisted audit techniques, and so on
- fieldwork techniques
- other assurance provider support
- audit assessments
- clearance meetings.

Measuring performance

- KPIs
- performance against KPIs
- measures used.

Marketing the IA function

- perceptions of Internal Audit
- the approach taken to market the function
- marketing documentation (if any).

Audit files, procedures and records

- audit file structures
- audit manual
- other policies
- audit methodology
- time recording.

The Audit Report

- structure
- format
- brevity
- clarity
- distribution
- the Executive Summary
- the main report
- action plans
- timescales for finalisation
- method of issue
- use of graphics
- recommendations implemented
- repeat findings
- use of positive language
- the review process.

Documentation to have available

Charter, terms of reference, and so on
Audit manual
Mission statement
Customer surveys
Key performance indicators or other measures used
Comments by management, director survey results
Partnered services and reports produced
Budgets and costs
Qualifications, skills assessments, training records
Records of starters and leavers in last 12 months
Audit plans – strategic and tactical
Audit programmes (three or four examples)
Records of assignments
Planning system
Two or three recent assignment files
Audit Committee reports (last two–three)
Management reports
Outline of recent investigations (if any)
Ideas for change
External Audit reports
Five or six audit reports – topics as diverse as possible

Estimated number of days for this phase – 3.5 days

Phase 2   Interviews with key Personnel

The interviews will be held concurrently with the review of documentation in Phase 1 interspersed with the meetings.

The personnel to be interviewed will be determined in conjunction with management but as a minimum should be:

Head of Internal Audit
Audit managers – including phone interviews with foreign-based management
Senior auditors
Chairman of the Audit Committee
Director to whom IA reports

Ideally short meetings should also be established with:

Chief Executive
Other Directors
Other regular senior recipients of Internal Audit reports

Estimated number of days required for interviews – 2.25 days

Phase 3   Preparation of Report

The information will be collated and evaluated and two reports prepared – one an Executive Summary and the other a detailed report.

The report will be organised as follows:

* Executive Summary;
* overall benchmarking score – out of a possible 400 including the relative overall position compared to other functions in the BRM database, for example, which quartile Internal Audit currently occupies;
* introduction and objectives;
* personnel interviewed;
* a separate section for each area reviewed (as highlighted earlier in this proposal). For each area reviewed strengths, opportunities and recommendations will be highlighted.

Estimated number of days for this phase – 3 days

Phase 4   Discussion of Report with Head of Internal Audit

After report has been issued and digested by the Head of Internal Audit a meeting will be held to discuss the report in depth and agree actions to be taken and timescales for implementation. The report will be updated to incorporate this information and a final report issued.

Estimated number of days for this phase – 1 day

Phase 5   Presentation to Audit Committee/Senior Management

This optional phase will incorporate the preparation and delivery of the key observations, recommendations and actions agreed for the Audit Committee or Senior Management.

Estimated number of days for this phase – 1 day
(NB If both presentations are required a further 0.5 day will need to be added)

3   PROJECT MANAGEMENT APPROACH

The project will be managed using a linked series of interviews and review of all documentation. All information gathered will then be used to score the service against best practice – comparing the practices with our global database of over 3300 internal functions (covering all sectors).

Each series of activities are evaluated in turn and a score given – with opportunities for improvement identified where necessary.

Part of the Business Risk Management Ltd Internal Audit benchmark scoring system is shown below:

Business Risk Management Ltd
Internal Audit Benchmarking Scores

	Possible	Actual
INTERNAL AUDIT CHARTER		
Charter in place	5	
Reviewed recently	1	
Issued widely	1	
Available on the Intranet	1	
Role adequately covered	1	
Authority explained	1	
Independence stressed	2	
Reporting line covered – and is appropriate	2	
Management's responsibilities incorporated	1	
TOTAL FOR THE SECTION	15	0

Professional standards for Internal Audit

Both the code of ethics and the IIA standards have been formally adopted	5	
This adoption incorporated in the Charter	1	
Someone responsible for monitoring – and has been done recently	1	
2004 update checked to ensure no compliance issues	1	
Evaluation of integrity	3	
Evaluation of objectivity – lack of bias in reports, raising issues, and so on	3	
Evaluation of confidentiality	3	
Evaluation of competency	3	
Assurance that the collaborative approach adopted by modern IA functions does not compromise its independence	3	
Evaluation between the balance, compliance, assurance and consulting aspects of the role	3	
Evaluation of exercising due professional care	2	
CPE development demonstrated	2	
Internal QA assessment process	2	
External QA assessment	3	
Planning – risk based	3	
Resource management – ensuring adequate resources	2	
Policies and procedures in place	2	
Board reporting	3	
Risk management evaluation	3	
Maintaining effective controls	3	
Governance assessment	3	
Engagement planning	3	
Engagement objectives	1	
Engagement scope	1	
Work programmes	2	
Performing the engagement	3	
Communicating results – criteria for communicating	3	
Quality of communications	3	
Disseminating results	1	
Monitoring progress	1	
Management's acceptance of risk	2	
TOTAL FOR THE SECTION	74	0

4   WORK PROGRAMMES

Work programmes for each section are used. As an example:

Questions	Responses	Comments
1.1 INTERNAL AUDIT CHARTER		
1 When was the Charter established?		
2 When was it last reviewed?		
3 Who authorised the Charter?		
4 To whom is it issued?		
5 Is it available on the Intranet?		
6 What do you think of it? What changes would you make?		
PROFESSIONAL STANDARDS FOR INTERNAL AUDIT – specific questions are included in each subsequent section.		
1 Have both the code of ethics and the IIA standards been formally adopted?		
2 Is this fact incorporated in the Charter?		
3 How is it ensured that all requirements are met?		
4 Who is responsible for monitoring?		
5 Have you checked that the 2004 update has not created any compliance issues?		
6 How do you ensure integrity is maintained?		
7 Some would say that the more collaborative approach being adopted by modern IA functions could compromise its independence. How do you ensure that this does not happen?		
8 How do you ensure your auditors remain completely objective?		
9 How do you balance the compliance, assurance and consulting aspects of the role (as per the standards)?		
10 How do you ensure that the auditors exercise due professional care?		
11 What internal QA assessments have you carried out?		

12 How do you ensure that you have adequate resources?		
13 Are you aware of performance standard 2600 – resolution of management's acceptance of risks? How have you applied this new standard?		
THE AUDIT COMMITTEE AND THE INTERNAL AUDIT RELATIONSHIP		
1 Describe the Internal Audit/Audit Committee relationship.		
2 How often does the Audit Committee meet?		
3 Are any of the meetings for IA exclusively?		
4 Does the Head of IA meet with the Chairman of the Audit Committee one to one? How frequently?		
5 Describe the membership and their individual attitudes to IA?		
6 What challenges have been issued by the Audit Committee?		
7 How have they been met?		
8 Have there been any areas of conflict or disagreement?		
9 What does the Audit Committee want to see? Audit reports – full or summaries?		
10 How does the Audit Committee assess IA performance?		
11 What is the format of the (quarterly) report to the AC?		
12 What feedback has been received?		
13 What opportunities are there to strengthen the relationship?		
14 What type of annual assurance statement are you required to make? What format does it take? Is it risk based?		

Section 9: Frequently asked questions

Q.   *What is Internal Audit?*

A.   Internal Audit is an independent and objective assurance function that assists the company to accomplish its objectives by evaluating the effectiveness of the internal control, risk management and governance processes.

Q.   *What are Internal Audit's responsibilities?*

A.   To assess risks, controls policies, systems and procedures and to report whether they are being managed effectively across all functions of the business.

Q.   *Why do we need IA?*

A.   Because an effective IA function can assist management to ensure that:

1   Risks are being appropriately managed.
2·   Records are reliable in order that management decisions can be based on accurate information.
3   The organisation's policies, procedures and instructions are being followed.
4   Inefficient or uneconomic operations or activities are identified and improvements made.
5   Assets are safeguarded.

Q.   *What line management responsibility does Internal Audit have?*

A.   None. Internal Audit is independent of all line management and therefore all activities that it audits.

Q.   *Why is it important for IA to be independent?*

A.   This ensures that the function is totally impartial in the work it carries out. It has no vested interests.

Q.   *Are Internal Auditors professionals?*

A.   Yes, the Institute of Internal Auditors was established in 1941 and all members have to adhere to professional standards. Group Internal Audit has adopted these standards.

Q.   *What right of access does IA have?*

A.   The Internal Audit Department may communicate directly with any Director or employee of the company and its subsidiaries and with any supplier or customer of the company.

Members of the department have the right of entry to all sites, works and offices and any other property if they consider it necessary during the conduct of an audit.

The department has unrestricted access to all books, records and documents (including computer files). However, a holder of highly confidential and sensitive information is entitled to insist that only senior audit management shall have access to it.

Q.   *Where do ideas for audits come from?*

A.   There are many sources. Internal Audit, taking into account the risks identified by management, prepares a plan of key activities and the risks and opportunities associated with them annually.

In addition, ideas for audits come from:

1   The Board of Directors
2   The Audit Committee
3   Line Management
4   External Auditors

Q.   *Does this mean I can request an audit?*

A.   Yes, most certainly.

Q.   *Will I receive advance notice of an audit?*

A.   Yes, the Audit Manager responsible will make contact to arrange an initial planning meeting four to five weeks prior to the scheduled commencement date of the audit.

Q.   *What can I do to facilitate the audit?*

A.   Understand the scope and objectives of the audit.
           Extract or have available the information required (a schedule of such information will be provided at the initial planning meeting). Ensure the most knowledgeable personnel in the area to be audited are available. Provide information when requested.

Q.   *How does Internal Audit decide what work to do?*

A.   In a disciplined and analytical way. The work to be carried out is planned in advance taking into account the relative importance of each activity and any changes in structure or personnel within the function or at the location. The auditor first determines the procedures and controls in operation (or any recent changes that have been made) and then carries out sufficient checks to determine whether these disciplines are being followed and also makes an assessment of whether the controls are appropriate.

Q.   *How does IA review controls?*

A.   By tracing documents through the system, also by speaking to staff, by observing how things are done, and reviewing operating instructions and procedures.

Q.   *What if controls are not applied?*

A.   The auditor will consider the impact of the situation and determine a practical solution in conjunction with the line manager responsible for the function or location.

Q.   *Are audit observations a question of judgement?*

A.   No. Internal Audit deals in facts. The methodical approach followed will also ensure that any Internal Auditor should be able to repeat the work of another auditor and arrive at similar conclusions.

Q.   *How are the results of the audit reported?*

A.   By discussion with the management of the function or location and more formally through the Audit Report which is distributed to both the manager responsible and senior management. All Audit Reports are circulated to the appropriate Board Director and are summarised twice a year for presentation to the Audit Committee.

Q.   *Will IA offer solutions to problems?*

A.   Yes, definitely. The published Audit Report will contain constructive recommendations designed to help management correct or minimise the effects of the problems identified. Management agreement with the recommendations will also be recorded in the report.

Q.   *Who is responsible for deciding what action is taken on Audit Reports?*

A.   Normally the manager responsible for the function, system or location in conjunction with the auditor. However, if agreement cannot be reached on a major issue, Internal Audit will refer to senior management, and if the issue is very significant, to the Audit Committee.

Q.   *What is External Audit?*

A.   EXTERNAL OR STATUTORY AUDIT is carried out by xxxx. Their role is to verify to the shareholders that the accounts of the company present a true and fair view of the organisation's financial position. It is a statutory requirement that the company accounts are audited annually by an external firm of accountants.

Q.   *Does External Audit work together with IA?*

A.   Yes, whilst responsibilities are different and are carried out independently, both plans and reports are shared and the External Auditors rely on the work carried out by Internal Audit when forming their opinion on the accounts.

Q.   *Can you summarise all this?*

A.   Yes.

Internal Audit is a service to management. It is independent and unbiased. It has wide powers but no line responsibilities. It is professional and thorough and above all constructive and practical. It is a key management control which functions by evaluating the effectiveness of the risk management, internal control and governance processes in the business.

Section 10: Misconceptions about the Internal Audit role

It is Internal Audit's job to identify fraud

No, Internal Audit attempts to minimise the risk of fraud by identifying failures in the procedures and weaknesses in control that might enable fraud to be perpetrated. This work sometimes results in fraud being detected and reported, in which case full investigation will be carried out.

Auditors are only interested in increasing controls

No, all controls cost money and the cost of achieving control must be balanced against the effects of things going wrong and the likelihood of this happening. Internal Audit will identify and report unnecessary or uneconomic controls as part of its review.

Internal Audit assesses the ability of managers or staff

Normally no. Internal Audit reviews the controls in operation, not the performance of individuals operating them or responsible for them. The auditor will, however, share concerns with management if significant loss, waste or risk is being caused due to the actions of, or lack of action by, a specific employee or employees.

Auditors can provide training if required

No, but we often do identify training requirements and make the appropriate personnel aware of these needs in order that training can be organised.

There is a set of mandatory requirements determined by Internal Audit

There is no such thing as an audit requirement – there is, however, a series of business policies and procedures that must be adhered to, for example, the financial risk and control manual.

Section 11: Chief Executive's Internal Audit brochure introduction

In any organisation, the responsibility for ensuring that corporate goals and objectives are achieved and that results are consistent with expectations rests with its management. To improve performance and ensure that the business delivers value to its shareholders in today's competitive and complex environment, management must take significant commercial risks. It is essential, therefore, that where risks are taken there are also adequate controls in place.

It is for this reason that we have a processional Internal Auditing function to monitor the effectiveness of risk management and controls, and assess the extent to which business processes are effective and contribute to the achievement of corporate goals and objectives.

Internal Audit provides a valuable service by advising on the relationship and balance between risk and control, thereby helping to ensure that:

- decisions are based on reliable and accurate information;
- assets are safeguarded;
- pocedures, laws and regulations are complied with;
- resources are used effectively and best practices are shared.

This document sets out the Terms of Reference of the Internal Audit function and outlines its objectives, status, independence and the scope of work carried out. It will demonstrate how you can contribute towards, and benefit from, the work carried out by Internal Audit.

Chief Executive

Section 12: Pre-meeting with management

This schedule should be used to plan the pre-meeting with management and to record the discussions. The attendees, audit planned and functional objectives (if known) should be completed prior to the meeting together with the audit objectives, scope and estimate of time on site. The sections following the table below provide a checklist of the questions and issues to raise. The threats, concerns, changes since last review and additional areas to consider should be completed at the meeting.

Attendees	*	
Audit planned (inc. suggested timing)	*	
Functional objectives	*	
Threats to their achievement (risks)	*	
Concerns and issues raised	*	
Changes since last review	*	

Additional areas to consider	*	
Audit objectives	*	
Scope (inc. areas to be excluded)	*	
Estimate of time on site	*	
Personnel to interview	*	

CHECKLIST OF ISSUES

Mission, strategy and objectives

- purpose and objectives of the function;
- where it fits in the organisation, who are the main managers;
- what the objectives are for the medium and long term, what has been achieved so far.

Internal, external factors
- Which specific items will facilitate or complicate the achievement of the objectives?
- What is the culture, leadership style within the function?
- How is the Internal Audit relationship with management, what are our experiences (do they always tell everything or do they hide things, and so on)?

Risk management
- Describe the risk management procedures and give a brief summary of risk assessment documents.

Processes, policies, procedures, resources and internal organisational structure
- Describe the key processes, policies and procedures and who are involved.
- How is the department organised?
- Are there any issues with staffing level, how well developed is the HR part of the organisation, and so on?
- Make reference to any documents in the permanent files.
- Which business/audit cycles have we identified?

Information and communication and monitoring and supervision
- Describe the way in which management communicates to the staff, the objectives, how they analyse the results, and so on.
- List the management meetings held and ask for the minutes.

Change projects
- Discuss all current projects: IT, business process redesign, new contracts, and so on.
- Include the scope, time horizon, current status, current results and resources allocated to the projects and the sponsors.

External audit
- Include any comments External Audit have made over the years for this organisation.

Section 13: Control objectives questionnaire

8–10 = Green   5–7 = Amber   1–4 = Red

2	PROCUREMENT OVERALL SCORE	6
2.1	Request for goods and services Section score	7
2.2	Product specification and supplier selection Section score	4
2.3	Maintenance of vendor standing data Section score	8
2.4	Raising purchase orders Section score	4
2.5	Receipt of goods and services Section score	6
2.6	Processing purchase invoices Section score	7
2.7	Creditors/accounts payable Section score	6
2.8	Payment to suppliers Section score	7

2	PROCUREMENT	
2.1	Request for goods and services Section score	7
2.1.1	Request for goods/services are authorised in accordance with the procedures	7
2.1.2	Goods/services requested are checked to ensure they are bona fide	8
2.1.3	Adequate segregation of duties	6

2.2	Product specification and supplier selection	4
2.2.1	Specification and quality of goods ordered is in accordance with those requested	5
2.2.2	Correct/economic qualities are ordered ensuring an adequate supply of critical materials	4
2.2.3	Suitable suppliers are selected in accordance with pre-determined criteria	4
2.2.4	Price considerations are properly factored in to ensure good value for money	3
2.2.5	The balance between quality, quantity, price and vendor selection is optimised	4

2.3	Maintenance of vendor standing data	8
2.3.1	The ability to amend standing data is suitably restricted	8
2.3.2	Amendments are properly authorised	8
2.3.3	Amendments are accurately processed	7
2.3.4	There is adequate segregation of duties	8

2.4	Raising purchase orders	4
2.4.1	Purchase orders are raised with the appropriate detail	4
2.4.2	Purchase orders are authorised	8
2.4.3	Purchase orders and contracts comply with applicable laws and regulations	7
2.4.4	Adequate segregation of duties	3

2.5	Receipt of goods and services	6
2.5.1	Goods are inspected on receipt and receiving reports prepared showing quantities and conditions of goods received	6
2.5.2	Receiving data is matched with purchase orders and any differences investigated	6
2.5.3	Damaged goods, late deliveries and returns are dealt with promptly	5
2.5.4	Goods received are handled in compliance with applicable laws and regulations	7

2.5.5	Details of services rendered are recorded at the time they are rendered	7
2.5.6	Adequate segregation of duties	6

2.6	Processing purchase invoices	7
2.6.1	Supplier invoice data for goods received is checked and matched with supplier order and receipt data	8
2.6.2	Supplier invoice data in respect of services rendered is checked and matched with underlying documentation. Confirmation is obtained that the service has been satisfactorily rendered as required.	8
2.6.3	The mathematical accuracy of supplier invoices and credit notes is checked together with account codings	9
2.6.4	Allowance is made for all returns and other similar credits, for example, containers, pallets, off-specification goods, and so on	7
2.6.5	The company avails itself of prompt settlement discounts, rebates, and so on, where available	4
2.6.6	Input VAT/sales and use taxes and duty on purchases are determined and accounted for in accordance with applicable laws and regulations	6
2.6.7	The supplier invoices for goods and services received are approved for payment in accordance with the Delegation of Authorities laid down	8
2.6.8	There is adequate segregation of duties	7

2.7	Creditors/accounts payable	6
2.7.1	Transactions are recorded promptly, accurately and on the correct purchase ledger account	9
2.7.2	Amendments, adjustments and delegations to ledger values are appropriately authorised	9
2.7.3	The debit balances are identified, controlled and collected	3
2.7.4	Payments are not made to suppliers who are also overdue debtors (in reciprocal trading situations) without appropriate authorisation	3

2.8	Payment to suppliers	7
2.8.1	Payments are prepared completely and accurately only on the basis of approved invoices or other supporting documentation	7
2.8.2	Discounts and translation of foreign currency payments are accurately calculated and properly recorded	8
2.8.3	Payment terms are agreed and approved in advance	8
2.8.4	Payments are approved in acccordance with the authorities laid down	8
2.8.5	Payments that are made by cheques are mailed promptly to the correct payee	7
2.8.6	Suppliers are paid at the correct time	5

2.8.7	Payments are made electronically using banking software and the privacy and integrity of payment data is maintained throughout downloading to disk or transmission	7
2.8.8	There is adequate segregation of duties	7

CONTROL OBJECTIVES AND AUDIT TESTING

The control objectives from the control objectives questionnaire should be entered with your evaluation of how well the objectives are being met. The audit tests to be completed should then be entered. The results of the tests should be recorded and potential Audit Report topics. The final column should be used to create the cross references to supporting documentation.

8–10 = Green   5–7 = Amber   1–4 = Red

Control objectives	How well are they being met? Score	Testing	Results	Audit Report topics	Reference to supporting documents/files
Product specification and supplier selection	4				
Specification and quality of goods ordered is in accordance with those requested.	5				
Correct/ economic qualities are ordered ensuring an adequate supply of critical materials.	4				
Suitable suppliers are selected in accordance with pre-determined criteria.	4				

Price considerations are properly factored in to ensure good value for money	3				
The balance between quality and vendor selection is optimised	4				

Section 14: Internal Audit Report template

Cover page (if you need one)

NAME OF BUSINESS TO WHICH AUDIT RELATES

INTERNAL AUDIT REPORT No. XXXX

TITLE OF AUDIT

DATE OF AUDIT

Report Distribution (but this is much better psychologically at the back of the report)

Final Report Distribution	cc
As draft	as draft + Board Director
Functional Director	Managing Director/Chief Executive
	Chairman of Audit Committee
	External Audit partner

Report prepared by   Auditor's name

Report approved by   Audit manager's name

Date of issue

Audit title – Internal Audit Report xxxx

EXECUTIVE SUMMARY

One page maximum.

Free format.

Brief overview of the objectives of the audit (two sentences maximum).

Now get the key message you want the Board, senior management to hear – hit them between the eyes – you want their attention.

Avoid descriptions of what you did (senior management are not usually interested).

Get as much praise and positive strokes in to ensure no overreaction or witch-hunting.

Demonstrate that management fully recognise the actions needed and are fully behind them.

Summarise the key actions.

Demonstrate that you understand any difficulties – support management – and that the actions are practical.

Quantify the issues raised if you can to demonstrate the value added by the audit but don't try and score points.

Include a photo or chart if relevant.

Be fair and objective.

Do not duplicate any of the wording in the main report.

Audit title – Internal Audit Report xxxx

MAIN REPORT first page

OBJECTIVES

The objectives should be as the published terms of reference (TOR).

Objectives should be short and sharp (two–three maximum).

An explanation of any changes to the objectives during the course of the audit should be given if appropriate.

No section on background should be included – management already know this or don't care.

SCOPE

Scope as TOR

Four to six bullet points to outline what was covered.

Avoid the words 'the scope included' – this just makes the reader wonder what was not included.

AUDIT OPINION

A discursive, short and to-the-point opinion related specifically to the objectives.

Avoid traffic lights or other scoring systems if you can. Tell management how it is – but make sure it is backed up by facts and is fair and impartial.

Make sure it's your opinion and not one you have been fed by management.

CONCLUSIONS

The conclusions should represent the key issues highlighted by the audit.

Get as many positive comments as you can in first.

Each conclusion should be a short separate paragraph (there should generally be no more than four).

They should flow logically in order of importance (as should the rest of the report).

Stick to the facts.

SENIOR MANAGEMENT COMMENTS

In format 'I ...'

Audit title – Internal Audit Report xxxx

1. MAIN REPORT (pages 2–5)

1.1   Avoid indexes if you can (but do number sections and cross reference to action plan).

1.2   Four pages maximum.

1.3   Headings should indicate the function, process, system or other audit area.

1.4   Keep sub-sections simple (numbering as here – avoid a, b, c or i, ii, iii).

1.5   Avoid words such as acceptable, satisfactory, reasonable.

1.6   Do not waffle or include great detail of what you did – explain the context, particularly the risk involved and then state your observations and the implications.

1.7   Refer to strategic objectives to put the findings in context.

1.8   Include photos, graphics and charts to illustrate the points.

1.9   Do not criticise people directly or by implication.

1.10   Praise efforts taken.

1.11   Refer to the future impact of the issues raised – if there is none do not include the finding at all.

1.12   Avoid reference to findings last time the audit was completed (unless this is a very positive outcome). Unless critically important take recurrent findings off-line.

ACTIONS AGREED

1   Actions should be numbered (sequentially – overall not within sections).

2   Actions should be concise and focused.

3   They should where possible indicate what will be achieved as a result.

4   If for any reason an action cannot be agreed, show under the heading of 'Recommendation' and explain after detailing the point that management have not accepted it (and demonstrating your understanding of their viewpoint, why you still believe that the issue is important and what action you will be taking, for example, Audit Committee).

MANAGEMENT COMMENTS (Joe Bloggs)

A short statement from a named manager directly related to the point.

Do not include word for word, if voluminous, but always agree any amendment you need to make before issuing the report.

Encourage positive feedback (for example, re value added if you can).

ACTION PLAN

Report Ref	*Agreed Actions*	To be implemented by		*Status*
		Whom	**When**	
1.9	An action plan should be completed in the same sequence as the report and attached as an appendix. The objective of the action plan is to summarise the agreed recommendations and to: a) indicate who has agreed them and is responsible for implementation; b) indicate a date by when the action is to be fully completed; c) provide a record for follow up by both management and yourselves. The actions should be cross-referenced to the main report. The action plan status should be updated when followed up (and can be used as the follow-up report).	Name and job title of person who has agreed the action and, if different, the name of the person responsible for implementation.	Date agreed for full implementation.	Record of the status of the action.

Index

About the Author

Phil Griffiths established Business Risk Management Ltd in 1999 to provide training, consulting and facilitation services to both the private and public sectors in the field of risk management, Internal Audit and fraud prevention.

He is passionate about the potential of Internal Audit and risk management as business enablers.

His company now has over 800 clients in over 25 countries. During the past six years Phil has personally trained over 10 000 people. He has advised many renowned organisations, co-ordinated top-level events and addressed national and international conferences on a wide range of critical business topics.

He has published many papers and articles in professional journals including 'The expectations of Chief Executives towards Internal Audit and its future' and 'How to optimise assurance'.

The core services provided by Business Risk Management Ltd are:

Training

- Together with a panel of expert associates, the company provides a wide range of open and in-house training courses covering all aspects of Internal Audit, risk management and fraud.
- The training experience is guaranteed to provide delegates with the very latest tools, techniques and ideas on each of these critical topics.
- Our most popular courses include:
  - risk-based auditing;
  - introduction to Internal Audit;
  - 100 ways to improve your audit reports;
  - embedding risk management into the corporate culture;
  - fraud – the invisible enemy.
- Details of these and the full range of training options can be found on the Business Risk Management website (at the bottom of the next page).

Risk Management Consultancy

- A facilitated workshop-based approach with the objective of enabling any organisation to quickly and effectively evaluate or review the significant risks impacting its operations and future direction.
- The process used is comprehensive but simple to understand and apply – it is therefore extremely cost effective.
- Services are tailored specifically to meet clients' exact requirements.
- Clear, comprehensive and timely output will be delivered with action plans that can be immediately put in train.
- Hundreds of organisations across all sectors have benefited.

Internal Audit services

- Benchmarking against worldwide best practice. This can be sector specific if required, that is, comparisons against others in the same sector as the client. It can also be completed as a peer review, as required every five years by the Institute of Internal Auditors.
- Practical advice of how to co-ordinate services with the other assurance providers such as Health & Safety, Insurance, Compliance and External Audit.

Fraud prevention, detection and investigation

- helping clients to understand the types of fraud their organisations are exposed to;
- trends and statistics regarding detected fraud can be compiled;
- researching sector specific case histories;
- building a picture of the major fraud risks – by facilitated workshops;
- building awareness of the most significant fraud indicators;
- how to spot the danger signals;
- examining powerful controls to mitigate the risks identified;
- introducing effective anti-fraud policies;
- developing fraud awareness training programmes;
- communicating standards of expected behaviour and ethics;
- how to manage investigation effectively.

To contact Phil to discuss any aspect of this book or to explore development opportunities:

E-mail: pg@businessrisk.co.uk

Phone: +44 161 339 3898

Fax: +44 161 339 9016

Website: www.businessrisk.co.uk

If you have found this book useful you may be interested in other titles from Gower

Corporate Fraud 3ed
Michael J. Comer
0 566 07810 4

Investigating Corporate Fraud
Michael J. Comer
0 566 08531 3

Statistical Sampling and Risk Analysis in Auditing
Peter Jones
0 566 08080 X

Managing Communications in a Crisis
Peter Ruff and Khalid Aziz
0 566 08294 2

How to Keep Operating in a Crisis:
Managing a Business in a Major Catastrophe
James Callan
0 566 08523 2

Buying Information Systems
Selecting, Implementing and Assessing Off-The-Shelf Systems
David James
0 566 08559 3

Security Manual 7ed
John Wilson and David Brooksbank
0 566 08174 1

GOWER

Join our e-mail newsletter

Gower is widely recognized as one of the world's leading publishers on management and business practice. Its programmes range from 1000-page handbooks through practical manuals to popular paperbacks. These cover all the main functions of management: human resource development, sales and marketing, project management, finance, etc. Gower also produces training videos and activities manuals on a wide range of management skills.

As our list is constantly developing you may find it difficult to keep abreast of new titles. With this in mind we offer a free e-mail news service, approximately once every two months, which provides a brief overview of the most recent titles and links into our catalogue, should you wish to read more or see sample pages.

To sign up to this service, send your request via e-mail to info@gowerpub.com. Please put your e-mail address in the body of the e-mail as confirmation of your agreement to receive information in this way.

GOWER